Praise for *Those Who Dared*

During the last half century, five heroes changed how we think about, lead, study, and organize American education. Their stories are powerful reminders that individuals can make a difference.

—Donna E. Shalala, President of the University of Miami, former U.S. Secretary of Health and Human Services, and recipient of the Presidential Medal of Freedom

Those Who Dared teaches us lessons beyond even the extraordinary work and lives of its authors—Henry Levin, Deborah Meier, James Comer, Ted Sizer, and John Goodlad. Their personal stories inspire us and remind us that this calling—the field of public education—is a process of becoming and of renewal or transformation. These men and woman are indeed giants in our time. How fortunate we are to have their "learnings" become ours and to see how passionately they believe in the "local-ness" of real educational excellence. . . . This book is a joy to read; it inspires one to go the next step—just as these remarkable leaders have done and continue to do every moment of their lives.

—Anne L. Bryant, Executive Director of the National School Boards Association

Warm, personal, straight-from-the-heart testimonies by five distinguished educators who are also intensely likable and just plain decent human beings. It is the endearingly autobiographical candor of these writings and the self-effacing and continually self-questioning humility of the authors that give this volume its unique appeal. I hope it will be read and treasured as a gift from these veterans to those of the younger generation who will carry on their struggle for democratic education in the frontline trenches of our public schools.

—Jonathan Kozol, author of *Letters to a Young Teacher* and *Amazing Grace*

These five people are all visionaries, to be sure, but even better for us readers, they are among the most talented writers to be found in the academy of education scholars and reformers today. It is a thrill to absorb these vivid accounts of their early years and see where their best ideas came from.

—Jay Mathews, education columnist for the *Washington Post*

For all those eager to pursue the seemingly endless battle to improve our nation's public schools, *Those Who Dared* is essential reading. The rich and challenging recollections of its five main contributors provide an outstanding blueprint for educational change at a time when obstacles to effective reform can often loom larger than life. My admiration for James Comer, John Goodlad, Henry Levin, Deborah Meier, and Ted Sizer is exceeded only by my hope that the lessons they teach us about what can be accomplished in the classroom will truly inspire a new generation of school leaders.

—Wendy D. Puriefoy, President of the Public Education Network

At a time when teaching, learning, and the very purpose of education are being defined so narrowly, this book reminds us of what schools can be: human and humane, intellectually vibrant, and deeply democratic.

—Mike Rose, author of *Possible Lives: The Promise of Public Education in America*

An insightful collection of essays by some of the most innovative and influential educational leaders and thinkers of the last 40 years. For those who are skeptical of the narrow focus of current school reform efforts, this book will be a refreshing source of inspiration.

—Pedro A. Noguera, Ph.D., Executive Director of the Metropolitan Center for Urban Education at New York University

This book is a treat and a gift. Most of us won't have the opportunity to spend a relaxed evening listening to Ted, Debbie, Jim, John, and Hank reflect on their journeys, and that makes reading *Those Who Dared* the next best option.

—John Merrow, education correspondent for the "NewsHour with Jim Lehrer" and President of Learning Matters, Inc.

Both practitioners and scholars will find the careers and personal journeys of these five latter-day progressives filled with insights into the past half-century of school reform. Their stories underscore the strong social, political, and economic links between the nation and its public schools and their valiant fight to make schools intellectually demanding, equitable, and democratic—tasks beyond the reach of so many current business-admiring reformers.

—Larry Cuban, Professor Emeritus at Stanford University and co-author of *Tinkering Toward Utopia: A Century of Public School Reform*

This is a book about all-American grit and intelligent determination. In it, we hear from five visionaries—a Harvard Dean turned school principal, a Yale psychologist and a Stanford economist turned school reformers, a kindergarten teacher and a one-room schoolhouse–teacher—all of whom became determined activists on behalf of better schools. Together, they sound a collective trumpet to remind us that it is critical that every child in America be well-educated. They demonstrate through their own experiences that this is not easy, that success requires complex solutions rather than simple strategies. Through the stories of their lives and work, they convince us that our schools have a huge role in the renewal of our nation and that each of us must work relentlessly to continue to pursue that ever-so-important and distinctly American dream.

—Pat Wasley, Dean of the College of Education at the University of Washington

Cutting against the grain of prevailing beliefs and practices, each of these remarkable leaders courageously challenged the status quo and created new ideas, practices, and institutions. Forever refuting the claims that "nothing can be done," they created new facts on the ground with vivid and unforgettable reforms. For the first time, we have their personal accounts to guide and inspire future educational pioneers.

—Lee S. Shulman, President Emeritus, Carnegie Foundation for the Advancement of Teaching and Charles E. Ducommun Professor of Education Emeritus at Stanford University

This slender volume packs a powerful punch: conveying, in very personal terms, the life lessons of five of American education's most towering figures. Anyone concerned about the democratic promise of public schools should read this book.

—Richard D. Kahlenberg, author of *Tough Liberal: Albert Shanker and the Battles Over Schools, Unions, Race and Democracy*

Those Who Dared

*Five Visionaries
Who Changed American Education*

Edited by Carl Glickman

Teachers College
Columbia University
New York and London

Please note that the contributors to this book have donated all royalties to non-profit organizations serving youth.

Published by Teachers College Press, 1234 Amsterdam Avenue, New York, NY 10027

Library of Congress Cataloging-in-Publication Data

    Those who dared : five visionaries who changed American education / edited by Carl Glickman.
        p. cm.
      Includes bibliographical references.
      ISBN 978-0-8077-4916-6 (pbk. : alk. paper)
      ISBN 978-0-8077-4917-3 (hardcover : alk. paper)
      1. Educators—United States—Biography. 2. Education—United States.
  I. Glickman, Carl D.
      LA2311.T53 2009
      370.92'2—dc22   2008032898

ISBN 978-0-8077-4916-6 (paper)
ISBN 978-0-8077-4917-3 (cloth)

Printed on acid-free paper
Manufactured in the United States of America

16   15   14   13   12   11   10   09   8   7   6   5   4   3   2   1

Contents

·◞

v

Acknowledgments

It has been an honor to be the editor of *Those Who Dared: Five Visionaries Who Changed American Education.*

I would like to thank Debbie Meier, Hank Levin, James Comer, John Goodlad, and Ted Sizer for agreeing to contribute their chapters to this book. They knew full well that I would pester them immensely and incessantly to write deeply and to divulge personal details, and they did so while having to surmount hectic travel schedules, serious illnesses, and great personal loss. My admiration for them—already over the top—continued to grow over the time we worked together on this project, and, at the end, all they wanted to know was whether their chapters would be helpful to a new generation of education leaders. Since words can't express all the gratitude that I have, all I can do is simply say to them, "Thank you for contributing to a memorable book whose lessons about education, change, and the human commitment to a public calling, will remain forever."

Next, I wish to acknowledge my friend George Wood, who wrote the conclusion to this book while also serving as full-time principal of two schools and carrying out the ongoing responsibilities of Executive Director of our policy group, The Forum for Education and Democracy. I also want to thank those who helped immensely in moving this book along through the many stages of its development: in particular Nancy Sizer, Linda Darling-Hammond, Paula and Tim McMannon, Cheryl Criscuolo, and Sara Glickman, all of who were adept at suggesting ideas and ways to proceed with different aspects of the book.

Teachers College Press has once again shown their mettle as a publishing house eager to take a chance on books that push the boundaries of conventional acceptance. The talent of the staff—Carole Saltz, Shannon Waite, Leyli Shayegan, Beverly Rivero, Nancy Power, David Strauss, Mike McGann, Emily Ballengee, and a host of others—is great, and the pride they take is apparent in the quality of the book from text to layout to illustrations to marketing. Shannon Waite, once again, has been my production editor par excellence and a joy to work with.

Finally, I wish to thank my colleagues in the Education Administration and Policy Program at The University of Georgia—Ron Cervero, Denise Collins, John Dayton, Elizabeth DeBray-Pelot, Suzanne Hall, Eric Houck, April Peters, Cathy Sielke, Max Skidmore, Cindy Williams, Sheneka Williams, Bill Wraga, and Sally Zepeda—who hired me back for a wonderful 3 years and provided me with the necessary collegial and clerical support for the making of this book.

Those
Who
Dared

June 1974: On the last day of school concluding his first year as supervisory principal of Hilltop and Chandler Elementary schools in Somersworth, New Hampshire.

Circa 2007. Reading to his granddaughter Quinn.

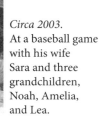

Circa 2003. At a baseball game with his wife Sara and three grandchildren, Noah, Amelia, and Lea.

Carl Glickman

•‿

Introduction

Carl Glickman is President of the Institute for Schools, Education, and Democracy and recently held the University Professorship at The University of Georgia, Athens. In 1990, he founded the nationally validated Georgia League of Professional Schools.

Carl began his career as a Teacher Corps intern in the rural South and later was a principal of award-winning schools in New Hampshire. Carl currently serves as a convener of The Forum for Education and Democracy and is a steering committee member of The National Campaign for the Civic Mission of Schools. He is the author of 13 books on school leadership, educational renewal, and the moral imperative of education and was the editor of *Letters to the Next President: What We Can Do About the Real Crisis in Public Education* chosen by *ForeWord* magazine as one of the two outstanding books in education for 2004.

Carl and his spouse Sara reside in Athens, Georgia, and spend summers talking, walking, reading, and fishing with children and grandchildren at Sara's ancestral home in northern Vermont.

What a pleasure to see this book come to fruition! What you, the reader, will find here is a candid and personal collection of new writings by Deborah Meier, James Comer, Hank Levin, John Goodlad, and Ted Sizer. Not only are they authorities on educational change, they are students of American society and its place in the world. Each has inspired hundreds of K–12 schools to incorporate the most powerful conceptions about the roles of education, schools, and community into their work with parents, teachers, students, and others. What makes this group the rarest of breeds is their unique combination of scholarly intellectualism and decades of unstinting activism in sustaining core ideas about the role of education in creating a more vital democracy. These authors have kept their heads in the clouds of ideas while planting their feet firmly in practice.

Over the course of their lengthy careers, Deborah Meier, John Goodlad, James Comer, Ted Sizer, and Hank Levin have dared to change the face of American education in spite of state-level and national movements that sought to usurp the power and decision making of schools. They have fought against the current technocratic, top-down standards and testing movement. The contributors' influence has been immense in the areas of creating small schools, performance assessment, developing comprehensive and rich curriculum, reorganizing student and teacher learning environments, and measuring student learning through exhibits and demonstrations. These leaders have a bold vision of the educated American student as a wise and engaged citizen rather than a competent test-taker, and they have repeatedly shown the power of schools that engage in thoughtful and purposeful practice.

Deborah Meier, James Comer, Hank Levin, John Goodlad, and Ted Sizer have dared to stand up to federal and state policymakers who wish to achieve school change from uniform, top-down mandates and single-test accountability requirements. Rather than arguing with those who seek to "improve" schools through use of power, authority, and control, these five visionaries simply responded by showing how ordinary people can create extraordinary schools when given a respectful climate of support centered around core principles.

This one-of-a-kind book brings together personal and evocative stories by critically influential and progressive educational leaders of the past half century. This book is both a call to further action as well as a personal illustration of the challenges and struggles of sustaining a rich and comprehensive form of education. The book serves as a guide and teaching tool and is appropriate both for readers who have followed the contributors' work and for those who are new to the field but are ready to take on the same challenge of building better schools and communities and educating a wiser, more participative citizenry.

Future history books covering the field of education in the last 50 years will acknowledge the impact of these individuals, and the next generation of educational leaders—students, teachers, administrators, academics, and activists—will benefit from the legacy of the lessons they have learned, which they set forth in these pages.

I know all of these writers well; they have been my professional mentors, friends, and colleagues. They do not think of themselves as heroes, and, I believe, rightfully so. They have the greatest respect and reverence for the real heroes of education, those teachers and other school-based leaders who support the public purpose of education in their daily work with students. This book came to be because I had a nagging concern about the passage of time and the need to capture the personal stories and lessons that these authors had told to me over the course of their careers.

I remember sitting in front of our wood stove in New Hampshire in 1974 when, as a principal of a progressive public school that was in the midst of a controversy about our team teaching and open classroom plan, I read a book by **John Goodlad** about his League of Democratic Schools. His guidance gave me the research base and psychological support I needed to develop our school curriculum and move to multi-age placement of students. Goodlad's subsequent studies on schooling in America, published in his book *A Place Called School,* found that parents and citizens desired schools that helped children to grow up to be wise and good citizens. Goodlad has been the lead proponent for a sustained nationwide agenda of initiatives and partnerships around democracy and education. His work has set the stage for the type of renewal needed at all levels of the education enterprise.

I first came across the name **Deborah Meier** in the mid-1970s when I read a *New York Times* article titled "The Little School That Could." This article was about an amazing small public school in Harlem, New York, called Central Park East. The activist principal, Deborah Meier, had collaborated with teachers and parents to create an oasis of hope in a struggling city school system. Her work was instrumental in starting the small school movement in New York (and later in other major cities), and she showed how education could be successful when children have a critical thinking curriculum focused on "habits of mind." Her book about her schools, *The Power of Their Ideas,* became a landmark guide for school change based on the best of progressive education ideals.

In the mid-1980s, while I was at the University of Georgia collaborating with secondary schools, I heard of a new study and book entitled *Horace's Compromise*. It was written by **Ted Sizer**, who would later use his findings and recommendations to form the network of high schools known as the Coalition of Essential Schools. The book described the life of a decent and highly committed teacher named Horace who was trapped in a traditional high school structure that prevented him from providing the quality of education that he knew that every high school student needed. Sizer recommended changing the standard, fragmented classroom environment of the typical secondary school, with separate courses taught by teachers in isolation, to an environment based on an intellectual core with longer classroom blocks; teachers and students working in small, stable teams; and student graduation requirements based on their performance on long-term projects and public demonstrations of learning. This book ushered in the greatest rethinking of the American High School since the 1950s, and the results of this work are seen today as large high schools across the country continue to be remade into smaller learning communities.

Later in the early 1990s, I was drawn to the work of **Hank Levin** when my colleagues and I developed The League of Professional Schools in Georgia. We had read of a professor of education and economics who had implemented a network of schools known as the Accelerated Schools (see Levin's book, *The Accelerated Schools Resource Guide*). We borrowed from his notion that the quality of education traditionally reserved for "gifted and talented" students should be provided for all children. Instead of remediation for underachieving students, consisting of skill-and-drill exercises and much passive seat work, he advocated providing them with a rich, exciting, and engaging curriculum. His work turned schools on their heads by paraphrasing John Dewey's thinking that the best education for the few must be the best education for all and that anything else is unlovely and detracts from a democracy. His work propelled new thinking about how all children have gifts and talents and curiosities to learn that mainstream schools have historically overlooked.

Finally, **James Comer** and I met around 1995 when we both served on the steering committee of Kids Voting USA, an organization devoted to engaging youth and parents in studying the issues of an open and civil society and teaching young Americans how to vote and participate constructively in their communities. Before I met him, I was already very familiar with his work and admired how he had created a distinctively holistic and proactive method for educating students. By the time we met, Comer already was a legend. This quiet man had used his medical background and insights as a psychiatrist to create the Child Development School Model—known by all of us in the field as the Comer School Model—wherein schools became hubs of caring for a student's developmental needs by partnering with health and social agencies and involving parents, teachers, and members of the larger community in determining how best to provide integrated services to the child. Comer felt that the quality of a student's life outside of school is as important as the quality of education received inside the school and that schools should treat health, shelter, safety, recreation, leisure, and family needs as well as improve relationships among and between teachers, parents, community agents and students. As a result, students would come to school better prepared and more committed to learning. His work (as found in the book *Rallying the Whole Village: The Comer Process for Reforming Education*) became a national model of school change that made large inroads into schools throughout the United States.

Over the years, I have had the good fortune to be part of various conversations with each of these five authors, in groups and individually, while sitting in living rooms, rocking on porches, strolling through forests, and convening at professional conferences. What has always struck me, and what inspired me to ask them to write for this book, is how different those conversations have been from my conversations with many other education leaders and reformers. My conversations with the contributors in this book have always framed discussions of "what needs to be done in education" in terms of economic theory, the contexts of culture and norms, the history of education, social movements, political theories, psychology, religion, citizenship, and the role of community in schools. I always left these conversations with a better sense of the next steps to promote healthy schools, but I also left with a much better understanding of the world as a whole. With other groups of reformers, the conversations were devoted almost entirely to education research, school change, education policy, and implementation strategies. Most of the people in these groups were either high-level policymakers or university faculty, and rarely were any of them actually doing work in schools. These conversations were helpful in their own right, but fell far short of capturing both the larger picture of education's place in human society and the actual lived experience of schooling.

When I approached the authors to write for this book, I asked them to describe the human side, rather than the purely professional side, of what it takes to cross boundaries and lead major change in how we think about education, its purpose, and its practice. I have asked each contributor to include in his or her chapter a personal story— previously untold—about a particular event or quandary that involved tension, insecurity, and struggle and then to discuss what they learned about themselves and their discipline. As an editor charged with the delightful task of working with such great leaders, I wanted to give these writers the autonomy to speak from their hearts and from their minds. As an added bonus, my friend George Wood, a high school principal and author who stands with this group in intellect if not exactly in age, agreed to contribute the concluding chapter on where we can go from here in the collaborative work of making public purpose central to the reshaping of American education.

Each chapter reinforces why this work—as each individual interprets it—is more important today than ever before; explores what has been accomplished to this point and the challenges, promises, and necessary action ahead; and recounts personal stories of critical moments in sustaining such work. The authors write in a nonacademic manner and have chosen their own themes. Some chapters are very personal, some more political, and some more practical. The chapters deal with the hopes, realities, scale, sustainability, politics and policy, and the personal and professional costs of sustaining major school change.

The authors discuss their lives, their careers, the challenges they undertook, and their vision of American education. These leaders have altered the face of American education, ushering in a democratic conception of what education can and should be for every student. They laid the groundwork for expansive changes in learning, offering rich and comprehensive curriculum and assessment, creating small schools and learning communities, redesigning secondary and elementary schools, forming social and community partnerships that support each child, providing gifted education for all children, implementing school choice within public authority, and incorporating habits of mind into public school life. It is my hope that this book will be a treasure trove of knowledge and inspiration for all those who continue to forge the paths of education for an educated and free citizenry.

My charge to you as a reader is to enjoy your time with this rare group of authors. Some are approaching the latter part of their careers, others still have many more years to go, but each has a wealth of personal and professional experiences to be passed on to future generations of leaders in the human struggle to promote the purposeful and powerful education that is so vital to a participatory democracy belonging to all of our children.

Circa 2004.
Photo taken by Dody Riggs.

Circa 1969–1972.
Leading morning sing-along
in the hallway of PS 144, which
connected the pre-k, kindergarten,
1st-grade, and 2nd-grade classrooms.

Circa 1969–1972.
A moment of
pleasure inside
Debbie's A.M.
kindergarten
class at PS 144.

Deborah Meier

•↩

What I've Learned

Deborah Meier has spent nearly 4 decades working in public education as a teacher, principal, writer, and public advocate. The elementary and secondary schools she helped create in New York City and Boston serve predominantly low-income African American and Latino students, and these schools are considered exemplars of performance-based, home-grown standards. She is the author of popular books such as *The Power of Their Ideas, In Schools We Trust*, and *Many Children Left Behind* (co-edited with George Wood). She serves as principal emeritus of Mission Hill School in Boston, co-chair of the Coalition for Essential Schools, and is currently a senior scholar at New York University's Steinhart School of Education. In 1987, Deborah Meier was awarded a McArthur Foundation "Genius" Award, the first educator to be so honored.

It was the early, heady 1960s and I was immersed in raising three very young children and trying, simultaneously, to change the world. I was deeply immersed in civil rights work, peace activism, and helping to keep alive a small, democratic socialist group led by Mike Harrington. But I was also short of cash. So, based on what a neighbor on Chicago's Southside told me, I decided it would be "easy" to pick up $35 a day as a substitute teacher in public K–8 schools. It would work with my schedule; I could offer maybe 2 days a week while my kids were in nursery school and kindergarten. I only needed to take a few courses (which were in themselves interesting as an insight into "ordinary" schooling) and off I went.

I was dead wrong. Being a sub was the hardest thing I had ever done, and I was clearly a failure at it. But, rather than being deterred, both of these factors intrigued me. Besides, I also relished the chance to get more than a sneak peek of Chicago's mostly Black public schools.

After my second year as a sub, it was getting wearying. So, I accepted a job as a morning kindergarten teacher at the school that my own children attended (which was also mostly Black). Me, kindergarten? Well, it seemed an easier way than subbing to pick up a little money and to stay close to home. Besides, it was a small school (maybe 300 kids in grades K–6), and its teaching staff included a large number of local women who were full-time teachers and neighborhood activists. This was bound to be easier than subbing all over the city.

Despite the fact that I purposefully avoided being a babysitter in my youth and the fact that I refused to take a single education course (against the wise advice of others), I fell in love with kindergarten teaching and became fascinated with my fellow teachers. I had led a privileged life, attending progressive "independent" schools in New York City as well as Antioch and the University of Chicago. Taking courses at the local teachers college was my first exposure to more traditional public schooling and public school students. Getting my teaching certificate at the Board of Education was my first experience at being treated with contempt and condescension. Although my own children had already embarked on long "careers" in public, urban schools, it was utterly new to me. My twice-a-week exposure as a sub offered me a new insight into the nature of America's inequities, the difficulties in creating a truly democratic ethos, and building a movement for change. The public schools were a force, wittingly or not, for preserving the status quo.

I meant to see how, exactly, this might be changed. I wanted to know: What are the small, telling ways in which we reinforce the prevailing class structure in our schools, and how do we perpetuate various ways of imagining possibilities? How is it that so many hard working and devoted women tolerate being treated so shabbily in their schools and yet stick with teaching, year after year? Why are mothers so fearful and often angry when they come to the school door and hand over their loved ones to the mostly well-meaning staff within?

On a much smaller scale, life within the classroom, itself, grabbed me. It was a place of endless fascination and constant intellectual, social, and moral struggle and delight. My first post-subbing classroom had 35 4- and 5–year-olds and no assistant. Yet, my energy was inexhaustible. Even though I only taught for half a day, it was, quite frankly, always a full-time job. During my "off time" outside of the classroom, I scoured my home and neighborhood for interesting objects, read books that might be useful for my classes, and met with families in the school and neighborhood to better make sense of what I was seeing and hearing. Inside the classroom, I had my students dictate stories to me, and I created little books for them to read, which I then read aloud back to them. The kids' stories were full of wonderfully rich language, a fact which countered what I was being told about these "language-deprived" children.

My experiences in those first few years of teaching were central to my 42-year career in urban public schools. I would go on to teach Head Start in Philadelphia and kindergarten in Central Harlem, found a series of public elementary and secondary schools in East Harlem, and, finally, start the Mission Hill school in Boston's Roxbury neighborhood.

I have learned that poverty and racism have a powerful out-of-school impact on the lives of our children that school alone cannot "undo." In fact, undoing is not the task. The task of schools is to re-do schooling so that it meets the strengths that children of poverty bring with them, joining with their families to make sure that schools are the richest and most soul- and mind-inspiring places they can be. Almost all children come to school with their imaginations intact. And even where trauma or sensory deprivation has wounded them severely (which can occur with privileged children as well), what they require is more space for recuperation, not boot camps to further alienate them from their most human of aspirations.

There were many discoveries that I made in my early years of teaching. I discovered early on that standardized tests are the most deceptive of instruments which hide rather than expose the intelligence and capacities of children with societal disadvantages. Through careful and well-documented efforts, I learned that the kids I taught often gave smarter and more well-thought-out "wrong" responses to short-answer and multiple-choice questions than their middle class White peers. Whether we were talking about a 2nd-grade reading test or a 4th-grade math test, what was being "picked up" by students were abilities that had less to do with reading and math than educators assumed. Forty years later we can document some of this even on SAT questions!

I discovered early on that young boys, for reasons utterly irrelevant to my concerns, were doubly wounded in schools, for reasons both obvious and subtle. The earlier one sought to inculcate so-called "academic" skills, the deeper the damage, and the more permanent the "achievement" gap.

I discovered early on that the remarkable early independence that poverty requires of the young not only is rarely rewarded in schools but is often turned into a disadvantage, as are the other early skills that come from having to cope with a less accommodating (coddling) environment.

And on and on.

Alongside some of the most exciting progressive educators of the 1960s and 1970s, I had an opportunity to explore these discoveries and the questions that arose from them and to imagine how schools could be redesigned to better unleash the intellectual capacities of all children, starting with their natural talents for play and imagination, for invention and exploration, and for building and creating both material and abstract ideas. I came to see that the rigidities we criticized in their families—including harsher punitive measures—were often responses to a punitive and discriminatory world and a means to protect their children from authorities over which their families had little control. It may, in today's terms, be a maladaptive response—but who was I to say? Maybe the institutions of society needed to be changed before such adaptive strategies were dropped.

But, if I could create an alliance with their families, could I create a school that would, at least to some degree, allow us all to better utilize our intelligence in the raising of all our children? Was the kind of collegiality that was necessary to sustain me personally possible, and could it collectively produce something more than any one of us could produce in our own isolated classrooms? Collegial critiquing—a setting in which people were both supportive and critical of one another—was far harder than I envisioned, and more time consuming. The trade-offs in seeking such critique were also more open to question than I expected; in spending our time one way, we reduced the time available for other forms of professional growth and for attention to our own immediate classroom/student tasks.

There were, finally, trade-offs that I hadn't anticipated between a "staff-governed" school in which decisions were largely made collectively by the staff and a "family-style" school in which parents felt their voices were critically important. The cohesiveness and empowerment of one often encroached on the other, particularly with respect to parents, who had more obvious choices and a greater sense of "entitlement."

It would be untrue to say that I succeeded in all my dreams—even for the classrooms or schools I was most responsible for creating. But I'm not sure I expected to. I probably thought I'd at least come to know the right answers, even if they didn't become norms. Yet none of the above issues have been resolved—even for me. All are issues I wish I could tackle once again with the energy of my youth. Sometimes I regret I didn't stay put at the Central Park East schools instead of reaching for more grandiose schemes.

None of the schools I started were permanently protected from the standardizing influences that have surrounded them in the last 20 years. Above all, I never figured out how, in the world of here and now, such schools could survive without very particular conditions—strong godfathers, politically strong leadership, and a few key politically hep parents. Sustainability, short of revolutionizing the entire system to one's way of thinking or breaking free altogether of the public system, has eluded me.

In fact, it's the first school—Central Park East I—that has lasted, more or less "intact" in terms of its practices, the longest. Begun in 1974, it is still alive today, although some of its fundamental practices are now in question and may or may not survive its sixth principal, the third in the last 5 years. But for nearly 30 years it took on more of the fundamental challenges without dropping its continuity and tradition. Graduates returned as teachers and parents of students, and we all were able to keep in touch over the last three decades or more. The next three schools have had a harder time, although Central Park East II is still a popular and successful school and the third, River East, might still be if it had not run into a deep political crisis that led to the removal of the principal and, essentially, to the closing of the school itself. Central Park East Secondary School, in some ways the most radical and deviant of all the

CPE schools, survived—alas. Alas because after the first 12 or 13 years, it rapidly dropped most of the characteristics it was famous for and became a fairly traditional 9–12 school of last resort.

Many of the other schools in New York City that were modeled on the CPE schools still survive. Some have reverted to quite traditional practices, while others still resemble the founding dreams and practices. It's impossible for me not to feel pleasure and pride at what we did accomplish in the face of so many odds being stacked against us.

Some of my initial assumptions about education and learning have proven only partially accurate. I presumed that a strong community of parents and teachers working together would be nearly impossible to rend asunder, and that such a community could protect the school in times of trouble. The assumption might be true, but working together under adverse circumstances—above all if the formal leadership (e.g., the principal) has other intentions—is far, far easier said than done. The inequality of the power granted to the school's constituency and the power granted to the central system is too huge. Principals are, after all, far more "accountable" to the officials "downtown" than to their own constituents. And while parents and staff working together sometimes can remove a hostile or inadequate principal, even a friendly administration can eventually throw up its hands and say "enough." Meanwhile, teachers and parents, with their various other responsibilities, can also soon retire from the fight. Even if schools *can* select their own leaders—something which is not built-in to the process in New York City—sustainability is not guaranteed.

I read, with envy, the literature from my old independent New York City school, and I visit and talk to current students, and I wonder at how they have kept the dreams of their founders—those who built the Ethnical Culture schools in the 19th century—intact, nearly a century later.

Relationships to what I'll roughly call "downtown" required me to rethink some of my earlier assumptions, too. I had hoped, even in New York City, that I could focus 97 percent of my energy on the world within the school—kids, families, and staff. Given that the schools I was involved with were not closely defined by their physical borders, I didn't even need to play as much community politics as many other principals might. And given various favorable factors, I assumed I could play the "political" game only when I chose and that I could take risks that other principals seemed unwilling to chance. However, I also really wanted to "change" the world around me in New York City, so I was aware that these favorable factors often inhibited my effectiveness. "Oh well," others might say. "SHE can get away with, SHE has other resources, SHE. . . ." Often these claims were untrue. I had, for example, no additional resources at Central Park East I or II. But there was an "aura" around me that *suggested* I *did* have privileges—that I had contacts, that I "knew" powerful people. In fact, part of this "aura" was a sleight of hand on my part, and far more people can and do play it just as I did. You use whatever you can! But you pay a price for it, too, because it makes it seem more insuperable to others, if not unfair.

The offer to move to Boston came at a time when we in New York City lost the fight over designing a minisystem with more autonomy and accountability in New York City. We attempted to carve out 5 percent of the system's population—50,000 pupils—and create a "freed" learning zone. While the original proposal, funded by Annenberg to the tune of nearly $50 million, had been approved by the chancellor, school board, state commissioner, and union, it didn't survive two critical changes: a new city chancellor and state commissioner.

The "out of school" interlude between my time in New York City and my time in Boston, which included a year traveling around as a Senior Urban Fellow at the Annenberg Institute at Brown University, was interesting, but I missed the dailyness of school, with its three-ring circus of dilemmas, and, above all, I missed the sustained human contact with kids and adults. I was running out of good stories to tell, those anecdotes that particularly suit this or that Big Idea.

In 1996, Boston offered a few schools a chance to explore the same idea we had proposed for New York City on a smaller scale. I had already "retired" from my New York City work, so I accepted the challenge in Boston. A move to Boston seemed just fine, and this time I could work from inside the schoolhouse. I could start a school which would be exempt from most "downtown" rules and union rules as part of a network of Pilot schools. The offer also came from a superintendent and union leader that I knew from other national projects and assumed I could trust. I was sufficiently old enough (65) not to want to work as hard, and

I figured that with more freedom from "downtown," the job would be less anxiety producing.

I still had so many unanswered questions going back to my first years of teaching, and now I could focus my attention on those again. Creating waves was another matter; Boston already had an organization that was set up to do this and didn't need much from me. It was modeled after an organization we had created a decade earlier in New York City called the Center for Collaborative Education. So I took full advantage of the opportunity in this new setting to keep my eyes on the daily life of school while others handled "the system."

It was an extraordinary success, both Mission Hill and the Pilot School network. But they, too, are struggling with sustaining themselves under changed district leadership and retiring founding principals.

In short, there is a price for the forms of power that one uses to succeed—everything from legitimate and understandable envy and fear ("What's she out for?") to the less attractive but natural jealousies that seek to cover up a failure to exert some courage and independence oneself—some of which are there for anybody to grab. And such responses complicate life when one needs a favor, which inevitably happens, even for completely "private" schools. We are all embedded in the larger world, and every act sets off reactions. Life is full of compromises. It's a tautology. It's even part of what we need to teach kids about—the how-tos of compromise.

It's not an accident that the main office at Mission Hill was also my office, the staff office, the parent office, and the place where calls came and went and notes were written on the board—official and nonofficial. When kids were "sent to the office," I wanted it to be a learning experience. I wanted them to hear me talking to "downtown"—cajoling, arguing, conspiring. I wanted them to read the notes on our faculty blackboard about our comings and goings. (The kids at some point asked for their own board.) We added extra computers to the office to ensure that kids would have additional reasons to hang out there.

But of course, in my case, I chose a public and political stance because it combined my fascination with the actual life of the classroom and school—including each child and staff member within it—with my lifelong love affair with political democracy. I occasionally weighed the advantages of keeping a lower profile. I had a friend who did just that and ran a remarkably "different" kind of public middle school (grades 5–8) for over 30 years that was known only to those "in the know." But it just wasn't in me to keep a lower profile. From day one, I used the pen to express my educational ideas. I wrote friendly, accessible (I hoped) letters home to parents starting the year I taught kindergarten half-time in Chicago. I wrote weekly letters home in every role I subsequently played. From the start, I wrote articles about schooling for various non-teacher magazines—primarily for *Dissent* (a socialist magazine with a long history), *The Nation,* and so on. When I began to get concerned with the role of testing, I joined with others to form the North Dakota Study Group to examine and resist such forms of evaluation, began to speak on the subject around the country, and wrote a few pamphlets and booklets aimed at teachers and parents on the subject. Until I became a "real" principal, I was active in the UFT-AFL-CIO and wrote for the union press. I joined the initial founding board for the National Board of Professional Teaching Standards (which is where I met two future superintendents I served under). I was elected to my own local school board and had a chance to see the world from that stance. And on and on.

I was also lucky to be the recipient of a prestigious MacArthur award just after starting Central Park East Secondary School. Being marked as a "genius," rather than just a dedicated school person, was immensely useful in elevating the status of my opinions about the world of schooling. And I was fortunate to be part of several "movements" that I got swept into after the end of the civil rights and peace movements of the 1960s and 1970s. Lilian Weber and then Hugh Dyasi of the City College Workshop Center provided a kind of stimulation and excitement around ideas that many of today's teachers do not run into in the course of pursuing their professional development. Vito Perrone's response to Head Start testing initiated the North Dakota Study group, which was a mini-movement that gave us precious opportunities to argue and discuss ides that were not fashionable. Finally, a decade later, Ted Sizer's *Horace's Compromise* led to the formation of the Coalition of Essential Schools, a network of hundreds of schools throughout the nation where I felt "at home." And each of these led to other offshoots. From Weber I got to know Eleanor Duckworth's and Pat Carini's work, and our schools had the chance to see themselves not as lonely mavericks but as part of an important stream of thought with historic roots and well-established ideas.

So it was not entirely surprising that I was constantly frustrated by the claim that whatever I did had no political significance because it was the impact of my "unique" circumstances. It was as though "they" were purposely undermining my expertise and example by honoring my work, simultaneously sending the message that it couldn't be "generalized." In fact what I "did" might have required fewer compromises had I not had such a public life.

But we are all unique. I was neither the best student in any of the schools I attended, nor a remarkably good writer or stylist, and my political "connections" were as much pretend as real. Besides, as my best friends will attest, I have plenty of natural faults that made my work harder. It's *choosing* to see oneself as a "player" and giving oneself the luxury of being able to fail that I excelled in, if one wants to put it that way.

Far more of us can do that, in our own way, and we need to help one another do it, because what we do can be done to scale. We need to start from the premise that "doing it our own way" while also making one's work accessible and reviewable by the public can be a "system" with the potential to turn the unique into the general. If all good-to-great schools are unique, expressing the character of their place and particular people, than a good-to-great system has to start there. I was just plain lucky enough to be in the game when two such "systems" (District 4 in East Harlem and the New York Alternative School system) existed under Tony Alvarado and Steve Phillips. It took less subterfuge to build one's unique school with them around as protectors, although even then it needed a few others!

In the end, what it rests on is taking advantage of the particular circumstances one finds oneself in—and that, after all, is what we're educating for. The purpose of education happily is consistent with the struggle to create good schools—if we share that struggle with our staffs, families, and, above all, the kids. It needn't be as lonely as we sometimes make it.

Can these coalitions and paradigms from the past sustain a new generation of like-minded maverick reformers? Will they refashion it in ways that might at first seem disturbing to me, but will in the end emerge the stronger for it? Will these difficult trade-offs be met in ways I did not know how to do, or will the trade-offs themselves be new ones I never encountered? A new language will be needed, as so much of our language has been co-opted. For example, "school autonomy" and "empowerment" are terms that now exclude the ability of teachers and principals, and even many local school boards, to make decisions about the essentials of schooling. "Accountability" to one's public has virtually no connection anymore to one's immediate constituents; instead it is built upon a per-verted version of what is sold to us as "the business model."

Of course, in the end, each of us comes to this with a unique history and enters it at a unique time and place. We step into the stream of progressive education, which has roots centuries old, at a particular moment. Whether the current is faster or slower, the bottom mushier or harder, our own particular stance and stamina will be what we work from. I wish I could come back a century from now and see what others have made of the work we did, much as we took the work of the late 19th- and early 20th-century reformers and tried to refashion it.

Circa 1973.
Shortly after receiving
tenure at Stanford.

Circa 1959.
Captain of the track
and cross-country
teams at New York
University.

Circa 2008.
Hank Levin
and his wife,
Pilar Soler, in
Montmartre,
Paris.

Henry M. Levin

·⤳

"You Have High Metabolism"

Henry M. Levin is the William Heard Kilpatrick Professor of Economics and Education at Teachers College, Columbia University; Director of the National Center for the Study of Privatization in Education, a nonpartisan entity; and David Jacks Professor of Higher Education and Economics, Emeritus, at Stanford University. Previously, he worked as an economist at the Brookings Institution in Washington, was Director of the Institute for Research on Educational Finance at Stanford, and served as the Director of the Accelerated Schools Project.

Levin has held Fulbright Professorships in Barcelona and Mexico, is on the Guest Faculty at Beijing University, has been a fellow of the Center for Advanced Study in the Behavioral Sciences and the Russell Sage Foundation, has been the editor of the *Review of Educational Research,* and was the President of the Evaluation Research Society, which awarded him its Gunnar Myrdal Award. He also received the 2004 Outstanding Service Award of the American Educational Finance Association and is an elected member of both the National Academy of Education and the International Academy of Education. He has been a member and President of the Palo Alto, California, School Board and is President of the Comparative and International Education Society.

Levin is a specialist in the economics of education and human resources and has published 20 books and about 300 articles on these and related subjects. At present, he is doing research on educational reform, educational vouchers, cost-effectiveness analysis, costs to society of inadequate education, and educational privatization. His most recent books are *Privatizing Educational Choice* and *The Price We Pay.*

Although his mother was from a family of 10 children and he was one of six siblings, he limited himself to only five children. He begins each of his economics classes with a poetry reading.

·ﾠ

The establishment of a school reform project can look like an impersonal organizational undertaking. But, it is a very personal undertaking on the part of the individuals who conceive it and attempt to implement it. The Accelerated Schools Project (ASP) was born from my own thinking about the type of school I wanted for my own children—I have five—and then expanded to include what I would want for all children. At its heart was the transformation of existing schools to accommodate all students in classrooms with enriched learning—the type of classrooms often found in outstanding gifted and talented programs. In truth, I wanted all children to be treated as gifted and talented by identifying and building on their strengths rather than focusing on their weaknesses. The ASP motto was "Accelerate, don't remediate." From 1980 until 2000, the ASP dominated almost all of my waking hours as well as many of the hours that I was pretending to be asleep. It was a continuing source of elation when I saw its successful unfolding and witnessed children thriving under its activities, but also a major source of disappointment when the ideas did not take hold, were adopted only superficially, or resisted by those who liked the *status quo,* or were overturned, even when they were highly successful, by a new school administrator.

Initially, I envisioned a 30-year commitment of working with schools from the time of establishing our first pilot schools in 1986. At that time I was 47 years of age, hardly a young age for developing a complex set of ideas and putting them into practice in a large network of schools. Fortunately, I was able to spend about half of the allotted 30 years actively implementing ASP, ultimately working with regional centers to support about 1,000 schools in 41 states with 50 schools in Hong Kong and a few schools in Australia and Brazil. I didn't finish the full 30 years because of a serious health problem that arose in the late 1990s. As I approached the new century, my health began to deteriorate from a frenetic schedule of travel, fundraising, school visits, training, conferences, coaching, and organizational management. All the while, I had to maintain a challenging schedule of teaching, advisement, research production, and publication. The consequence of this demanding regimen was a case of heart failure, which forced me to withdraw from active involvement in ASP, although

I never lost my attachment to the concept nor my gratitude for having been able to participate.

This chapter represents a brief summary of the personal voyage that I took while establishing the Accelerated Schools Project, including some of the joys and challenges that I experienced along the way. It is not a detailed presentation of the ASP philosophy and process, which can be found in other publications (e.g., Hopfenberg, Levin, et al., 1993), but rather a more private account of my experience. I begin with a classroom visit in one of our two earliest ASP schools and proceed to a brief description of the characteristics of an Accelerated School. I follow this with the story of my own journey from receiving my Ph.D. in Economics to discovering my passion for school transformation and student learning. In the final section, I address some of the lessons that I learned along the way.

Why Do Bears Hibernate?

As I entered room 13 at Whittier School, Ms. Ronda was just lining up her second graders to go to the playground for recess. As they exited the room, I followed. Arnold, an endearing and active child, turned around and asked, "Do you have high metabolism or low metabolism?" I was startled by the question and assumed that he had heard a medical consultation where that question was asked of his mother. I said to him that I thought I had high metabolism, and he replied "me too" and ran off to play with his friends. I approached Ms. Ronda, and as we strode out toward the school yard I exclaimed excitedly, "Arnold knows the word *metabolism.*" Ms. Ronda responded, "They all do. It was part of our bear unit."

Ms. Ronda recounted how she and another 2nd-grade teacher had formulated their study of bears. They began by reading children's stories about bears, such as Paddington Bear and Winnie the Pooh, to the class. They proceeded to ask the children to draw the California State Flag, with its emblematic California Grizzly bear lumbering across its center. They recounted to the children the history of bears in California at the time of its settlement and the importance of the bear to the natives who occupied the territory. They also reported on the demise of the Indian natives and the decline of the bear and its habitat, simultaneously devastated by the settlers. The students began to compile a bear vocabulary booklet of words that the teacher wrote on the board in block letters drawn from the stories, history, and lifestyle of the bear. The children copied the words in their books and discussed in class the meanings from the contexts of the stories and teacher presentations. They saw videos of bears in the wild and their various life phases, including footage of the birth and nurturing of baby bears, hibernation, and typical bear diets. They calculated the food requirements of a family of bears by adding the different amounts of berries, fish, and grass the family in the video consumed for a day. They also compiled small booklets in which they drew pictures with crayon on one page and wrote a corresponding sentence, with the teacher's help, describing the picture and using their bear vocabularies on the facing page. These booklets were presented as gifts to their parents on parent day, demonstrating to parents that their talented children were already learning to write ideas and stories. The students had also taken a trip to the San Francisco Zoo, where a docent gave them a tour of the bear enclosure and answered their questions.

Finally, the class as a whole scripted a dramatic production of "Wooly," a story of a baby grizzly bear that got lost in the wild and had to find his family. The children offered ideas about how Wooly might feel about his dilemma and offered suggestions for how he could solve it, and the teacher wrote everything down in the form of a play. Roles were assigned to all of the children, including preparation of scenery. The children practiced for a half hour each day for over 2 weeks and presented the play to an audience of parents on Bear Day (also known as "parent day"). Bear Day was a culminating celebration. The children brought in toy bears (or were provided with them by the PTA), and the parents (mostly "Momma Bears") prepared "bear claw" cookies and honey lemonade with ingredients provided by the school.

I asked Ms. Ronda, "What did all of this have to do with metabolism?" She said, "Oh, I forgot. When Julie and I prepared the [unit on the] science of the bear, we wanted to emphasize how they ate too much and built up their fat and then went to sleep for the winter. But, when we began to read about the science of hibernation, it was not about sleep or gluttony. It was about the bear's surviving for the winter by the slow metabolizing of the fat that had been stored up. In the spring the bear emerges from hibernation, very thin and hungry after a long winter, and the metabolic process speeds up, necessitating that the bear must consume prodigious amounts of food. So, we decided to describe hibernation not as sleep, but as the slowing of the bear's metabolism, and the wake-up in the spring as a return to high metabolism.

To make the concept come alive, we asked the children to copy the word in their bear vocabulary, and we demonstrated the hibernation cycle by engaging the children in vigorous bear exercises (running in place) and then gradually slowing down and beginning hibernation. Then we played the sound of birds chirping in the springtime, and our little bears began to arise and yawn and stretch—and to return from their low metabolism phase to high metabolism. To cement the idea, we also asked if certain prominent persons had high or low metabolism. For example, we compared President George H. W. Bush (the elder) with Michael Jackson and asked which one had high metabolism and which had low metabolism. Then we went around the room asking the question about each student to see if we could get consensus. Finally, I asked them about me. Of the 24 children in the class that day, 23 of them raised their hands and said that I had high metabolism. I was gratified, but Keisha shouted out: 'You have low metabolism.'

I turned to Keisha and inquired, 'Why do you think I have low metabolism?' thinking that she did not understand the word or concept. She responded by imitating what she saw me doing yesterday at the end of class when the bussed kids got up to leave. Apparently, I sat exhausted at my table with my head supported by my hands and my mouth gaping with exhaustion from a long and active day. Keisha concluded: 'You had low metabolism.' We all laughed."

As we returned to Room 13, I was enthralled with Ms. Ronda's description of the second graders' encounter with the bear. The students had combined many subjects with very active learning and imagination and had reached for challenging words and concepts often thought to be beyond 7-year–olds' comprehension. In short, this was an enriched curriculum, one for treating all students as gifted and talented and curious learners ready to capitalize on their sense of wonder. This was precisely what we wanted to see in an accelerated school with an emphasis on unity of purpose, empowerment with responsibility, and building on strengths of student and teacher. I should also add that these students, largely minority and living in public housing projects, would likely never have seen the inside of a gifted and talented classroom.

But, even beyond the impact on the students, Ms. Ronda and her companion 2nd-grade teacher found the experience to be enriching for them. As they prepared the unit, they learned about the science of the bear and the parallels between the decline of the bear, the destruction of its habitat across northern California, and the decimation of the native population. Since they would address the Indian inhabitants of early California throughout the elementary school curriculum, the bear unit provided a useful connection to their future schooling. Both teachers told me that this unit and several others that they had prepared together had revitalized their love of teaching and made them feel that they were learning as much or even more than their students.

From the introduction of the ASP in Whittier School in 1986 to these events in 1988, we had seen a profound transformation of students, teachers, and parents—and of teaching and learning. As one of our first pilot schools, I was thrilled that after 2 years of hard work, the type of education my colleagues and I had dreamed about was showing promise, at least in the second grade of Whittier School. But, what did we dream of? We wanted every child to be valued for his or her strengths and provided with an enriched education that would accelerate the development of his or her skills, thirst for knowledge, love of learning, engagement in the arts, democratic participation, and ability to address the practical and conceptual challenges he or she would face in the future. Within ASP schools, every child was to be treated as gifted and talented and to be provided with an education that accelerated (not remediated) his or her growth and development. This was our dream.

A Personal Path

As an undergraduate at New York University, I focused on both business studies and cross-country running and track. By the time of my graduation in 1960, I had merited a track scholarship at NYU and had reached a national ranking as one of the top ten distance runners in college. I had also become increasingly attached to academic study and especially courses in the liberal arts. After returning home to New Jersey and working for a year to pay off debts, I decided to study for an M.A. in economics at Rutgers University. My initial plan was to return to an academic environment where I could do extensive reading and writing, rather than seeking a degree or career. However, the seduction of addressing complex social issues through research and the attention of a wonderful mentor, Professor C. Harry Kahn, induced me to undertake a Ph.D. in economics.

The 1960s ushered in a vibrant academic job market with many opportunities. Although tempted by several offers of faculty positions in economics, I chose to accept a research position at the Brookings Institution in Washington. Brookings had been at the vortex of the whirlwind of civil rights legislation during both the Kennedy and Johnson administrations, and I was attracted by these associations as well as its venerable research reputation. Upon joining the Economic Studies Division of Brookings in the summer of 1966, I was asked to conduct research in a new field, the economics of education. I lacked expertise on education, but had some background in the economics of human resources and labor economics. To integrate this academic knowledge with an understanding of practice, I took a position as a long-term substitute teacher in an all-Black junior high school in Washington, D.C. The experience of teaching math and social studies several days a week—I turned my compensation over to Brookings—impressed deeply upon me how repressive the schools were for poor Black students. The school routine was unpleasant; teachers communicated with students largely by shouting, admonishing, and commanding; and school routines were rigidly punitive for both students and teachers alike. I was reminded of these experiences often when I began to formulate the Accelerated Schools Project almost 15 years later.

The famous Coleman Report (Coleman, 1966) was published to great fanfare in my first week in Washington. This social science report, authored by Professor James S. Coleman, a sociologist at the Johns Hopkins University, at the request of the U.S. Office of Education (prior to the establishment of the U.S. Department of Education in 1980), the report collected and analyzed extensive data on the determinants of academic achievement.

It found large differences in student achievement at every grade level between White and minority students, favoring White students. More unexpected was the Report's conclusion that improved resources for poor and minority students would not redress this gap. The Report declared that disparities in such school resources as educational expenditures, teachers, class size, and facilities made little difference in explaining student achievement. Instead, it concluded that socioeconomic status (SES) was the most important determinant of achievement.

The sheer magnitude of the Coleman Report—with its 737 pages, very large data base of 600,000 students and 70,000 teachers, and sophisticated statistical analysis—made it an immediate landmark of educational debate and policy. Conservatives saw it as justification for not investing more money in the education of the poor. Liberals saw it as justification for school integration along SES and racial lines, claiming greater peer diversity would substitute for additional school resources. I saw the report as a reservoir of data to use for carrying out economic analysis and began to study the dynamics of teacher markets using the data on teachers and schools collected by Coleman.

In reviewing the data and statistical procedures used by Coleman, I was stunned by what appeared to be statistical flaws in the Report and contradictions between the Report's conclusions and what I had experienced in my substitute teaching. The educational conditions in my school were bad. Classes had about 35 students and were beset with student disruptions; there was high absenteeism and student mobility; the building was deteriorating, with cracked windows and poor ventilation; textbooks and instructional materials were in short supply; and teacher shortages and staff turnover were considered normal. While I did not see resources as the only problem, the disparities between our school resources and programs and those of the more affluent White schools to the west of Rock Creek Park were astounding.

When we began to analyze the Coleman data, we found that the research team had used a statistical method that consistently understated the impact of resource differences on student outcomes. For example, resources had been measured poorly, using district averages for per pupil expenditures at a time when schools in poor neighborhoods were getting much less investment than the district average and those in more advantaged neighborhoods were getting more. Class sizes were measured incorrectly, as well, because of a flaw in the questionnaire. I felt compelled to point out that more equitable resource strategies should still be on the policy agenda.

My friend Sam Bowles, who had similar concerns about the Coleman Report, and I began to criticize the Report's conclusions and to re-analyze some of the data. We circulated our rather critical paper among academics and policymakers, but were criticized by some for undermining the credibility of a report which also advocated school integration (a policy that we favored, too). We believed that many of the conclusions of the report were not supported by the evidence that was presented. We submitted our critique to four different journals and received rejections from all, often without any explanation other than a refusal to consider a critique of an iconic report. Finally, we submitted it to the relatively new *Journal of Human Resources,* where it was accepted and published— probably because it was a young journal and welcomed the attention that would be drawn from the controversy (Bowles & Levin, 1968). Both the pre-publication draft and the published version propelled us into being active players in the educational policy debates of that time, creating greater personal understanding of the issues and contacts with key academics, educators, and policymakers.

But something was happening in my private life that also began to challenge my personal goals and values. When I arrived in Washington, D.C., in July of 1966, I had wanted to do the best technical work possible in order to impress other scholars and eventually land a good position in a top department of economics. However, as I observed the great injustices in the treatment of minority and poor youngsters at the school where I taught, I developed a growing personal interest in changing these conditions. At the same time, I was living in a city that was the command center of an escalating conflict in Vietnam, a conflagration which I opposed strongly. With two children of my own at that time, I was pained by the agony of the napalm-bombed villages of people that were not a threat to us or "our way of life." I began to educate myself about the Vietnam War, and nothing that I learned justified the combat casualties and civilian suffering. I felt that I had to speak out against this abomination, and so I joined a group called Concerned Citizens for

Peace. Every weekend we walked the pavements of Washington, D.C., with signs opposing the war and went house-to-house asking residents to come to our meetings, which were held at local churches. We were often rejected and yelled at for being disloyal or worse, and soon my telephone line was subject to frequent bouts of dysfunction.

Gradually, I began to see that academic work with no personal commitment was not for me. I wanted to do work that would be highly regarded academically and in the world of practice, but I was becoming just as interested in working on issues of justice in education. When Martin Luther King Jr. was murdered in 1967, I became further radicalized.

Education was also becoming more polarized, with integration proceeding ever so slowly in response to the *Brown v. Board of Education* decision of 1954. By the end of 1967, the frustration of some D.C. citizens had created a national movement (along with the larger one in New York City) which sought to grant minorities community control of their neighborhood schools. The premise was that if the larger society was unwilling to integrate urban schools and provide them with appropriate resources, control of the resources, curriculum, and personnel of those schools should be shifted to the neighborhoods that were most affected by school operations. By coincidence, I hit it off with Kenneth Haskins, the Principal of the experiment in community control at the Adams-Morgan School, and he took me under his wing and gave me a front row seat to the fight. I visited his school regularly and attended meetings of his local board. I became so fascinated by this movement that I asked Brookings if I could put together a conference that joined activists, academics, journalists, and others to debate and discuss it. To my surprise, my supervisor supported my request, and, with Brookings sponsorship, I was able to convene The Brookings Conference on the Community Schools in 1968 and produce one of the first published works on the subject (Levin, 1970b).

But, by the fall of 1967, I had become thoroughly disillusioned with Washington, especially with its fading commitment to the War on Poverty and its rising commitment to War in Vietnam. As the controversial critique of the Coleman Report received more and more publicity, I started to get inquiries from universities about my future plans. One of these feelers came from Stanford University in California, and I began to dream of moving to California—a giant venture for one who had never been west of Fort Wayne, Indiana or south of Washington, D.C. I was invited to fly out to Palo Alto, California, for interviews, and I was smitten with the beauty of the area and its anti-War activism as well as the intellectual challenge of Stanford. I accepted the offer of a faculty position and waited impatiently to undertake my transcontinental migration. This escape from Washington took on even more meaning when, three weeks before I departed, our great presidential hope to end the war, Robert Kennedy, was assassinated.

Going West

In June of 1968, I arrived at Stanford to take up my faculty position in the School of Education with a joint appointment in the Department of Economics. The School of Education faculty and administration were not quite sure what an economist does or was supposed to do in a professional school. In the late 1960s, the economics of education was a new field. The novelty turned out to be an advantage for me because it meant that I could design my own teaching and research role. But, I now faced a new preoccupation on the future decision of my tenure. Discussions with my Dean and Department Chair suggested that they would lean heavily on evaluations from senior economists—not necessarily drawn from the nascent field of economics of education—to decide whether to grant me tenure. That worried me because I feared the tenure procedure would pressure me to do narrow technical and abstract work in an effort to impress other economists and distract me from my devotion to the social issues that were really important to me.

Within a few months of my arrival at Stanford, my third child was born adding to my sleepless nights and anxious days. I joined the teach-ins and protests opposing the Vietnam War and became a regular at the Peace Center established in Palo Alto by Joan Baez. I was teaching, doing research, participating in the anti-War movement, and unsuccessfully trying to keep a failing marriage together while taking care of three kids for much of the time. I also worried how my high-profile activism would affect my chances for getting tenure. Then, one day it dawned on me that tenure was not worth worrying about. If I was publishing good scholarship, focusing on social and educational issues of great importance, and teaching successfully—along with my many other responsibilities—that was all that I could do. If my colleagues and the university rejected me for tenure, clearly I was at the wrong place and should simply move on and find the right one. So, I forgot about tenure and just did what I thought was right.

Studies motivated by social issues were my first priority. During this period, I applied my focus on cost-effectiveness and cost-benefit analysis toward improving resource allocation and resource effectiveness for at–risk students (e.g., Levin, 1970a). I also undertook joint research with others to establish the first social science evidence in support of the legal challenge to the inequities in state education financing that short-changed the poor (Guthrie, Kleindorfer, Levin, & Stout, 1971), and I prepared a report for the U.S. Senate that showed that the social costs of inadequate education exceeded the costs of providing a decent education for all (Levin, 1972). Fortunately, a fairly high rate of publication led to my receipt of tenure in 1973 and a full professorship in 1975.

But, the casualties and costs of the war had ground me down psychologically and undermined my faith that democratic processes could produce a fair society. In the quest for a more hopeful outlook, I undertook a research project with a colleague, Martin Carnoy, to study the challenges of both democratic participation and its educational requirements. We wanted to explore ways of creating a more responsive democracy and greater economic, political, and social equity. This was a long-term project of international scope. We realized that schools were molding students to comport with two opposing political regimes, a democratic one encouraging free discourse and civic participation and an authoritarian one demanding obedience to workplace authority where even basic constitutional rights were proscribed. Students were being encouraged to value freedom of speech as citizens but to give up such rights when they undertook employment and entered the workplace. This appeared to us to be a complicated and contradictory way of developing healthy personalities.

So, we asked, "Why can't we create work organizations that are democratic, where workers elect their managers and participate directly or through representation in the major decisions affecting their working lives?" If this were to happen, we could integrate the political socialization of students by preparing them for democratic roles as *both* citizens *and* workers. We studied extensively several movements in Europe that gave workers greater voice in their work organizations. At the same time we contemplated how schools might change to become more democratic in their organization, relationships, teaching, and curriculum content. Although we published many articles on different aspects of this research in the seventies, it took a full decade for us to publish a book-length treatment on what we had learned in *Schooling and Work in the Democratic State* (Carnoy & Levin, 1985).

Simultaneously, I began to take an interest in a particular form of democratic workplace, the worker cooperative. Worker cooperatives are both owned and managed directly by their workers or through elected management. My colleagues and I studied worker cooperatives in the United States and abroad. I spent the spring of 1976 visiting Basque cooperatives in Northern Spain to understand their management, training, investments, productivity, worker pay and benefits, and educational preparation. At that time, these cooperatives were the largest producers of domestic appliances and many other products in Spain, with revenues of almost $700 million. (Total sales in 2003 were more than $13 billion, with employment of 68,000.) Robert Jackall and I combined our studies of worker cooperatives to produce a book that summarized the lessons learned (Jackall & Levin, 1984).

During the early 1970s, I had gotten a divorce and married my present wife of 37 years, Pilar Soler. She had lived in Spain, Colombia, and Venezuela, and she introduced me to the Spanish language and Latino culture and experience. I continued to ponder what the Vietnamese War had wrought on our society, including how it had undermined the War on Poverty. In 1978, I became the Director of the Institute for Research on Educational Finance and Governance (IFG), a federally-funded research and development Center at Stanford. The Institute was the official research center of the National Institute of Education and, later, the U.S. Department of Education for addressing the economics of education, educational finance, politics of education, and educational law and organizations. The IFG developed a very active focus on issues of poverty and education. Drawing on Stanford faculty in many departments as well as faculty at other universities, we were able to produce 50 research reports a year, most of them eventually published in books and journals. However, by 1984 the U.S. Department of Education had taken a rightward turn away from our equity agenda and chose not to renew funding in the areas that we covered. The subsequent demise of the IFG enabled me to work full-time on my preoccupation with the schooling of the poor—something that I had begun to contemplate in 1980.

The Accelerated Schools Project

With the exception of my spell as a substitute teacher in social studies in D.C., I had no direct experience working in schools. My research was focused primarily on the effectiveness of resources, finance, and organizational forms of schooling rather than on classroom dynamics. With the loss of funding for the IFG, I decided to go in a new direction. By the early 1980s, the War on Poverty of the middle 1960s had been largely forgotten. Educational reform in the United States was focused heavily on competing educationally and economically with Asia—particularly Japan—and Europe but was not really concerned about equity. Reports like the influential *Nation at Risk* (National Commission on Excellence in Education, 1983) spoke about the alleged mediocrity of the entire U.S. system of education. The slogan that "a rising tide lifts all boats" became a rallying cry, rather than singling out those boats most likely to founder.

In response, I undertook a study of education of disadvantaged students in the United States in terms of their changing demography, educational practices, educational outcomes, and social consequences. The resulting report defined disadvantaged students as those who were unlikely to succeed educationally in existing schools because they lack the experiences that schools value and build upon (Levin, 1986). About one-third of U.S. students met that definition, and the percentage was rising because of increasing rates of child poverty, single-parent families, and immigration from less-developed regions of the world.

This report emphasized that disadvantaged students began school with lower academic proficiencies and fewer experiences in the home and the community that support academic success in schools as they were currently constituted. The longer that they were in school, the farther they lagged the mainstream in academic results. I became convinced that the slow and less challenging forms of instruction utilized in remediation were at least partially responsible for this result. Thus, began a search for forms of instruction that might accelerate the progress of these children so that they would enter the academic mainstream within a few years and succeed educationally.

In addition to a review of the research on learning, I visited schools with high concentrations of at-risk students. I observed that classrooms in these schools were characterized by considerable repetition and memorization. Teachers following these methods seemed uninspired and were preoccupied with keeping order in a situation that lacked intrinsic motivation for students. Most of the classrooms lacked experiences which drew upon the imagination, previous experiences, curiosity, and creativity of students. Only in the few gifted and talented classes did I observe students mastering basic skills within a context of discussion, extensive writing, artistic endeavors, research projects, and collaboration. These latter classrooms vibrated with excitement, and teachers and students were immersed in work that appeared meaningful to them.

I concluded that conventional interventions for children who were educationally at-risk were unlikely to have more than a very limited impact in improving their achievement, and that they undermined the students' creativity, initiative, and capacities to develop insight and agency in real-world situations. Such conventional practices were premised largely on the remedial education model, which assumed that students must be saddled with constant memorization and repetition of low-level skills before they can be engaged and provided with more challenging activities.

I also concluded that it was not the type of remediation that was at fault as much as the whole concept of remediation. Although *remediate* is not listed as a verb in the English language, educators frequently use the word as a transitive verb—for example, "to remediate a student." The *Webster's New Collegiate Dictionary* (1979) defined remediation as the "act or process of remedying" where remedy is defined as "treatment that relieves or cures a disease" or "something that corrects or counteracts an evil" (p. 970). Presumably, children who are put into remedial programs are children who arrive at school with "defects" in their development that require repair. But the school repair shop is surely different than other repair shops in the sense that the children are rarely repaired. Rather they remain in educational repair shops for most or all of their education, whether they are labeled as Chapter I, LD (learning disabled), or any of the many categorical labels for educational defects. This, in itself, convinced me that programs which slow down the pacing and challenge of instruction and learning actually stunt the healthy development of the child. Although educational remediation was conceived with the best of intentions, one must judge it by its results. Once in the repair shop, children are stigmatized as permanently damaged goods, and they soon learn to view themselves this way for their entire educational careers.

The obvious solution seemed to be the opposite. If children arrive at school without the skills that schools expect, slowing down their development through remediation will get them farther behind. If all children are ultimately to succeed in the academic mainstream, we must accelerate their growth and development, not restrict it. This notion was further reinforced when I saw gifted and talented classes in these schools—students were identified according to their strengths and not labeled according to their weaknesses. Gifted students were celebrated for their talents, and their learning growth was palpable as these highly valued and stimulated students were continually motivated and challenged to think, reflect, create, perform, and master.

Starting in about 1984, I began to conjure a picture of a school that would accelerate learning through identifying the strengths of students and engaging them more deeply in building on their strengths through enriched activities. I submitted it to a few highly respected educators, such as my colleague Larry Cuban. The feedback that I received was basically positive, but there were some tough questions regarding how one can transform the culture of a school from remediation to acceleration, a transformation that went beyond what thoughtful experts thought was possible (Sarason, 1982). I added some details on transformation, but felt that I could not really answer that question without solid experience in working with schools. Larry Cuban sent my accelerated schools write-up to the superintendents of two local school districts, San Francisco and

Redwood City, and they graciously nominated schools that we could try to persuade to work with me and my team of graduate students to see how the accelerated schools ideas might unfold.

We devoted a considerable time to visiting Whittier School and Collier School on a regular basis to get to know the students and staff and the few parents who showed up. Both schools had a large majority of students who qualified for free or reduced-cost lunches, but the ethnic distributions were different. Over 90 percent of Collier's enrollments were drawn from recent immigrants of rural villages in Mexico. In contrast, Whittier's students were more evenly divided among Hispanic, African American, and Chinese American ethnicities with a small percentage of Anglos. At least half of Whittier's students were drawn from the local public housing project, which was known for crime and violence. With regular visits, it took most of the first academic year to get to know the schools and for schools' staffs to get to know what we meant by an accelerated school. During the second semester of that year, both schools voted to support the accelerated school model, and we began the long process of transformation.

Much of what we learned about school transformation in these two schools and subsequent ones is captured in our Resource Guide (Hopfenberg, Levin, et al., 1993). But, what is important to note is that the ASP model was one of continuous development; we would try different approaches and evaluate their results and modify them as appropriate. The school transformation process was a learning process that never ended, both for the schools and for us as their guides and coaches. Out of these experiences, we learned many lessons (Finnan, St. John, McCarthy, & Slovacek, 1995).

To a large degree I was able to build on my early work in organizational democracy and worker cooperatives. The schools that we sought were ones that enlisted a deeply democratic process of building a unity of purpose, taking responsibility for decisions and their consequences, and building on the strengths of all of the participants including the students, teachers, other school staff, parents, and community members. I mention this because the ASP approach and process are profoundly influenced by what I learned over the years leading up to the formulation of the model as well as what I learned during the implementation of the ASP approach.

The ASP change strategy represents a philosophy and a process for transforming conventional schools into environments where powerful learning experiences are daily occurrences for all members of a school community. The philosophy of the ASP encompasses an overall goal of acceleration for all, three core principles, a set of central values, and a theory of learning we call *powerful learning*. The ASP process is constructed to embrace participatory organizational theory as a framework for guiding a systematic set of practices designed to get from conventional schools to accelerated ones.[1] And it is all based upon the democratic participation in the Deweyan tradition.

Particularly central to building on student strengths is the concept of powerful learning, which integrates curriculum, instruction, and school organization rather than viewing each dimension as independent. Powerful learning is based on the premise that the educational approach that we create for "gifted" children works well for *all* children. It is important that students see meaning in their lessons and perceive connections between school activities and experiences outside of the school, to borrow from John Dewey. They should learn actively and in ways that build upon their own strengths, develop their natural talents and gifts, and apply them in creative ways toward problem-solving and decision-making. These learning experiences require higher-order thinking, complex reasoning, and relevant content. In such situations, children actively discover the curriculum objectives, rather than passively going through textbooks and filling out worksheets. At the same time, this type of learning environment requires organization and support, and adults are challenged to create a safe environment for learning that extends far beyond the classroom into every aspect of the school, home, and community.

Beginning with the two pilot schools in 1986, by the late 1990s we had reached more than 1,000 schools in 41 states, Hong Kong, and Australia. Although the process of school transformation was challenging and did not always succeed against deeply held traditions, the Accelerated Schools Project became one of the major school reform projects of its time. We worked primarily with traditional public schools, but we also worked with charter schools and Catholic schools. Indeed, one of the earliest charter schools in California, started in 1993 in south-central Los

Angeles, is called The Accelerated School, and it is one of the most successful charter schools in the state.

Unfortunately, there is no standard rubric used by government agencies suitable for evaluating an Accelerated School. Clearly, the garden variety of standardized testing is not appropriate. Nevertheless, an independent evaluation of Accelerated Schools by a nationally prominent evaluation organization found strong academic results on test scores at relatively low cost (Bloom et al., 2001). But, I saw these results—as Dewey would have—as a mere by-product of the educational process, rather than an instrumental goal.

Personal Lessons

On a more personal level, what did I learn from these many years of commitment to the development of Accelerated Schools?

Improving My Teaching. My many observations of powerful learning in classrooms and my participation in developing powerful learning lessons in our pilot schools transformed my own teaching. I discovered enormous possibilities for improving learning in my classes—and for improving my own learning. I began to use the same principles of powerful learning to examine my classroom purposes and activities and formulate lessons that were built more fully on the strengths and interests of my students and my passions.

Recognizing Talent. I found much more talent in the schools among teachers, students, other school staff, and parents than I had expected. Sadly, that talent is underutilized in a school environment that is focused on compliance and narrow accountability. The fact that so many talents, hobbies, and areas of personal strength of staff and parents go unrecognized and are even subverted as irrelevant is a terrible loss to the schools. The good news is that they emerge when democratic processes are used to formulate activities. School participants display—and even flaunt— their talents when they see how important they can be to educational purpose and practices. Participation in the ASP locates and enlists talent in addressing classroom and school activities. I also developed a deep respect for talented teaching and teaching practice, something which I had not recognized in the theoretical and statistical abstractions of an economist working on education.

Leadership. The ASP will not prosper in the absence of strong and supportive leadership. In most cases, this is a principal who understands the process, lives it, models it, and promotes it throughout every classroom and school activity. However, in some cases a principal with more modest understanding and leadership abilities will enlist strong teachers and other staff and bestow upon them leadership roles by distributing ASP leadership. Such leadership must be sustained, but is constantly under threat by appointment of a new principal or a change in district leadership. New appointees to these roles often seem to promote their identities by "bringing in their own ideas" regardless of the success of present practices. Occasionally, they pretend to honor existing reforms in words while undermining the values and practices on which they are based. School reformers have little control over changes in personnel or personnel selection.

Time. There is never enough time for planning, problem-solving, group learning, democratic participation in decisions, gathering information, celebrating, and all of the other activities that need to be incorporated into an Accelerated School. So called in-service days are few, and allocations for preparation time are typically encumbered by other demands that cannot be easily shed. Democratic decision-making for the school, problem-solving with inquiry methods, and the formulation and implementation of powerful learning units take considerable time, but all expand equity and effectiveness of instruction considerably. ASP always found that even creative ways of obtaining time outside of instruction was challenging and required compromises of personal time and school activities. Somehow we must find ways of building more time into the school day for planning and collaboration (as the Japanese do), even if there are fewer minutes of instruction.

Test Score Pressures. Even when school districts and school staff were supportive of ASP, they were tyrannized by the pressure to concentrate on subjects that were tested by the district and state forcing them to forego powerful learning with its broader focus. This has become a particularly serious challenge under the No Child Left Behind Act of 2001 (NCLB). Teachers feel that they have to constantly compromise their beliefs and values to meet testing pressures. Despite their commitment to ASP, the teachers in our pilot schools often had to put their own priorities on the back-burner to prepare students for testing. And in some schools these pressures occurred not just at test-taking time but for the entire school year, making ASP activities a luxury at best or contraband at worst.

Universities as Reform Platforms. Perhaps the worst strategic decision that I made was in launching the Accelerated Schools project from a university. Universities are wonderful institutions for developing reform approaches, especially if they are linked to a "laboratory" of schools in which one can test the ideas. But once it appears that the reform has merit, the university is not necessarily a good platform for developing, expanding, and sustaining a reform. There are many reasons for this. One of the most important is that a university is a competitor for resources. Project development and expansion requires enormous financial help that does not contribute to research publications and other types of public notoriety that universities seek. Universities want to see that a reform idea is associated with university research, but they do not want to provide for the care, nurturing, financial support, and risk of failure of that reform idea. Further, the very philanthropic sources that one must seek support from are the same sources that the development office of the university is also beseeching, and the symbolic authority of development officers and deans take precedent over sponsors of educational reforms when it comes to receiving funding from foundations.

Although no malice was intended toward ASP by Stanford University, the Deans of the School of Education were not interested in the project. As long as I paid overhead on any grants that I received and allocated part of the grant to pay a portion of my salary (freeing up those funds for use by the School for other purposes), no one interfered with the Accelerated Schools Project. But, at the same time there was no assistance in raising funds for supporting the project, nor was any financial assistance provided by either the School of Education or the University. In fact, the School of Education preempted funding from one foundation after I had been engaged in negotiations with that entity for several months and had submitted a proposal at its request. What happened was that the Foundation's key education officer called me to say that the grant had been approved by her staff, but her superior had just had a meeting with the dean of the School of Education at Stanford, who had submitted a list of priorities for funding of which ASP was not one. It should be noted that charitable foundations prefer that universities and their constituent schools set priorities that are coordinated institutionally rather than receiving myriad grant proposals from individual faculty that are not prioritized or supported by the parent institution. My request was not supported by my dean, and the willingness to fund Accelerated Schools was rescinded.

A final concern was my experience in establishing regional centers around the country to provide training, coaching, and support for their local Accelerated Schools. At the beginning, when we did not charge schools for training, I had to raise funds to establish these university-based centers. I asked the administrators at these institutions to appoint center directors who would receive training and launch pilot schools, and, subsequently select and train their own staff to support an expansion of accelerated schools in their regions. In some cases, the institutions nominated their least productive faculty in terms of teaching and research and attempted to convince me that they were appropriate. In other cases, they selected appropriate faculty, but many of those who were appointed used the training to do their own private consulting rather than build a productive Accelerated Schools center. In spite of our efforts to reinforce democratic ideals by engaging satellite directors as members of our overall governance body, the Accelerated Schools culture did not overcome this type of individual faculty consulting and other practices. In only a few of the 13 cases was there a deep commitment to the project where the schools' staffs devoted the kind of energy, development, and collegial collaboration that we had expected from satellite centers of ASP. In some cases, the universities that sponsored the satellite centers used the national reputation of ASP as bait for attracting funding that they used for other purposes.

At some point, we should have broken away from a university-bound organization with university-based satellite centers and established a more coherent and disciplined organization through a nonprofit educational entity. In that way we would not have had to compete with our university for funding or be subject to the whims of its priorities and its lip-service to the importance of improving educational practice. We would have been able to establish clear standards of operation that would have been shared by all of our members through consistent recruitment, training, and participation in the spirit of the Accelerated Schools processes and goals.

Transforming School Cultures

So much has been said about the resistance to change of school culture that I will not belabor the point here. I, myself, have written extensively about this obstacle and how to address it (Finnan & Levin, 2006; Levin & Finnan, 2000). However, it is important to state that school culture cannot be changed readily from the outside. You cannot simply provide a package of practices from external sources and expect schools to adopt them. The process of change must rely primarily on the internal transformation of school culture where the model of change is one that empowers rather than limits the participants' ability to consider the challenges facing the school and establish a unity of purpose; mechanisms for self-governance, democracy, and accountability; and exposure to powerful ways of improving learning. It is the internal transformation of school culture in the hands of the participants that is at the heart of accelerated schools, and this transformation must be implemented effectively if schools are going to create the rich futures that we desire for our children.

Colleagueship

I cannot stress enough the need for good colleagueship in moving forward the school reform agenda. I had some wonderful colleagues in this journey, from faculty like Larry Cuban and Ed Bridges, who encouraged me and saw the possibilities of ASP to the graduate students that accompanied me on the early phases of our project. Also, I must acknowledge the strong contributions of three of our leaders at the Stanford Accelerated Schools Center: Wendy Hopfenberg, Pilar Soler, and Kari Merchant. So much of the development of the ASP would not have happened if I had not been so lucky to have their assistance. Then there are those at our satellite centers and at school sites who provided the leadership, ideas, and innovations that influenced our direction—so many that I can not fully do justice by listing names. Without their colleagueship, I would have felt impoverished and isolated relative to the hungry demands of a national school reform. I must also give thanks to Jim Comer, Carl Glickman, John Goodlad, Linda Darling-Hammond, Debbie Meier, Ted Sizer, and George Wood for the inspiration emanating from them personally and through their respective school reforms.

Some Final Words

My active involvement in the Accelerated Schools Project ended in 2000 when a serious heart condition necessitated relinquishing direction of the Project. Because I had retired from Stanford, the Center was moved to another university that had actively sought it. I have not been contacted by that Center in several years, and mention of my role and that of Stanford University have disappeared completely from the materials and website of that Center. And, indeed, I have returned to my work on the economics of education (e.g., Belfield & Levin, 2007). However, I continue to reflect on my experiences and write occasionally on what was learned (e.g., Finnan & Levin, 2006). I continue to marvel on what was accomplished, with minimal resources and without institutional support, and feel pride when I hear about ASP schools that were established long ago which have sustained their efforts and success (such as The Accelerated School in Los Angeles). In many respects, my involvement with ASP was the richest professional and personal experience of my very long career, and I thank the vagaries of serendipity for having led me there. My close friend, the late Frank Newman, former president of the Education Commission of the States, always introduced me by saying that I became an economist because I lacked the personality to be an accountant. This may be true, but I found passion in Accelerated Schools.

Notes

1. A comprehensive presentation of ASP is found in the Resource Guide for the project, Hopfenberg, Levin, et al. (1993). A recent summary of what was learned in the project is found in Finnan & Levin (2006).

References

Belfield, C., & Levin, H. M. (Eds.). (2007). *The price we pay: The economic and social cost of inadequate education.* New York: The Brookings Institution.

Bloom, H., Ham, S., Melton, L., O'Brien, J., with Doolittle, F. C., & Kogehiro, S. (2001). *Evaluating the accelerated schools approach.* New York: MDRC.

Bowles, S., & Levin, H. M. (1968). The determinants of scholastic achievement: An appraisal of some recent evidence. *Journal of Human Resources,* Winter, 1–24.

Carnoy, M., & Levin, H. M. (1985). *Schooling and work in the Democratic state.* Stanford, CA: Stanford University Press.

Coleman, J. S. (1966). *Equality of educational opportunity.* Washington, DC: U.S. Government Printing Office.

Finnan, C., St. John, E., McCarthy, J., & Slovacek, S. (Eds.). (1996). *Accelerated schools in action: Lessons from the field.* Thousand Oaks, CA: Corwin Press.

Finnan, C., & Levin, H. M. (2006). Accelerated schools and the obstacles to school reform. In M. A. Constas & R. J. Sternberg (Eds.), *Translating theory and research into educational practice.* Mahwah, NJ: Lawrence Erlbaum.

Guthrie, J. W., Kleindorfer, G. B., Levin, H. M., & Stout, R. (1971). *Schools and inequality.* Cambridge, MA: MIT Press.

Hopfenberg, W., Levin, H. M., Chase, C., Christensen, G., Moore, M., Soler, P., Brunner, I., Keller, B., & Rodriguez, G. (1993). *The accelerated schools resource guide.* San Francisco: Jossey-Bass.

Jackall, R., & Levin, H. M. (Eds.). (1984). *Worker cooperatives in America.* Los Angeles and Berkeley: University of California Press.

Levin, H. M. (Ed.). (1970a). *Community control of schools.* Washington, DC: The Brookings Institution.

Levin, H. M. (1970b). A cost-effectiveness analysis of teacher selection. *Journal of Human Resources,* Winter, 24–33.

Levin, H. M. (1972). *The costs to the nation of inadequate education* (A report for the select committee on equal educational opportunity, U.S. Senate). Washington, DC: U.S. Government Printing Office.

Levin, H. M. (1986). *Educational reform for disadvantaged students: An emerging crisis.* Washington, DC: National Education Association.

Levin, H. M., & Finnan, C. (2000). Changing school cultures. In J. Elliot & H. Altrichter (Eds.), *Images of educational change* (pp. 87–98). Milton Keynes, UK: Open University Press.

National Commission on Excellence in Education. (1983). *A Nation at Risk*. Washington, DC: U.S. Government Printing Office.

Sarason, S. (1982). *The culture of the school and the problem of change* (2nd ed.). Boston: Allyn & Bacon.

Webster's New Collegiate Dictionary. (1979). Springfield, MA: G. & C. Merriam Company.

Circa 1985. At the School Development Program Pilot Schools Reunion Event, New Haven.

Circa 1959.
In his third year of medical school at Howard University.

Circa 2008.
At Yale University School of Medicine.

James P. Comer, M.D.

·‿

From There to Here

James P. Comer, M.D., is the Maurice Falk Professor of Child Psychiatry at the Yale University School of Medicine's Child Study Center in New Haven, Connecticut. He is known nationally and internationally for his creation of the Comer School Development Program, (SDP). He is the author of nine books, including *Maggie's American Dream,* and *Leave No Child Behind.* His pioneering work in school restructuring has been featured in numerous newspapers, magazines, and television reports and has been published in many academic journals. He is a co-founder, and past president, of the Black Psychiatrists of America. He has served on the board of several universities, foundations, and corporations. He was a consultant to Children's Television Workshop and has served as a consultant, committee member, advisory board member, and trustee to numerous local and national organizations serving children. He is currently serving on an NCATE National Expert Panel on Increasing the Application of Knowledge About Child and Adolescent Development in Educator Preparation Programs.

Dr. Comer has received 46 honorary degrees, including three in 2008 from Harvard University, Lesley University, and Sacred Heart University. He has been the recipient of many awards and honors, including the John and Mary Markle Scholar in Academic Medicine Award, Rockefeller Public Service Award, Harold W. McGraw Jr. Prize in Education, Charles A. Dana Award for Pioneering Achievement in Education, the Heinz Award for the Human Condition, and, most recently, the University of Louisville 2007 Grawemeyer Award for Education. He is a member of the Institute of Medicine and the American Academy of Arts and Sciences.

My first career goal was to become a general practitioner of medicine in my hometown of East Chicago, Indiana. Indeed, I got a head start by doing my internship in the local St. Catherine's Hospital. At the same time, I observed the downhill life path of three of my best friends from elementary school. What I observed and knew about them caused me to pause and eventually inspired me to go on a journey in search of understanding and in an effort to improve schools.

The four of us were African American youngsters whose parents were from the rural South, had low levels of education, and worked as steel mill laborers and domestics. We attended the same elementary, middle, and high schools. Our predominantly White school served working-class, executive, and professional families, and my three friends were as intelligent as anybody in my family and anybody in our school. My four siblings and I thrived in the school and eventually obtained 13 college degrees among us. Why were my friends not successful in school? Why was the school not successful with them?

Some African American students with similar backgrounds to me and my friends whom I met after late elementary school were successful in school and in life. But too many others with good potential were not. One of my three friends died early from alcoholism, another spent a large part of his life in jail, and the third was in and out of mental institutions until his death. Even some of my high school classmates who seemed destined for success either achieved far below their potential or went on a similar downhill course after their school years. What did it mean? Why were so many friends and acquaintances living in poverty and displaying dysfunctional behavior at a time when steel mill jobs still offered a living wage to most. What could be done?

The pursuit of answers to these questions turned me away from the practice of clinical medicine and led to a career in public health and preventive psychiatry, with a focus on schools and education. These questions have greatly influenced the work I have done over the years. They remain a guide and a touchstone as I work in an education enterprise that is full of activity which is supposed to address these questions but is not appropriately oriented or critically focused enough to do so. I will return to this point.

I temporarily retreated from the frontlines of medical practice, albeit gradually and with significant uncertainty and ambivalence. My father died 5 years before my internship, and my mother had sacrificed greatly to create "my son the doctor." I had a growing concern about social problems, but I also had a young family, no money, and a military service obligation. To give myself time to think about how to address these issues, I changed my plan for completing my military service requirement. Instead of serving in the National Guard part-time while starting my private practice, I chose to serve in the United States Public Health Service (USPHS). This allowed me to earn a living, think about my concerns, and explore my options.

In an attempt to be helpful and better understand the bad outcomes of good people, I got involved as a volunteer with a private "boot strap" community organization in Washington, D.C., called Hospitality House. Hospitality House served African American women and children who had been thrown off public welfare, usually because an official found a "man in the house." The mothers at Hospitality House had no money and few belongings. Getting health care and child care was fragmented (the mothers had to deal with many different organizations often in widely different areas), consumed large amounts of time and energy, and often involved disparaging providers. The children were bright and lively, but the schools were not serving them well. One penniless youngster was told by his teacher that, if he did not bring a dime back for the class Easter egg hunt, he should not come back himself. It struck me that society was providing more harassment than help to these families.

It was 1962 and the industrial era was all but over. Getting a living-wage job in the rapidly emerging high-technology, science-based economy required not only academic success but also good social, psycho-emotional, moral/ethical, linguistic, and cognitive skills. The children who passed through Hospitality House were unlikely to succeed in the new economy; they were more likely to end up like my childhood friends. This situation was not receiving adequate attention, much to the nation's peril. None of the easy explanations for this potentially destructive situation—race, class, and sexism—seemed adequate to me, and this piqued my interest. I decided to continue my exploration at the School of Public Health at the University of Michigan, while still a USPHS officer.

If things did not work out, I could still return to private practice and serve as a local part-time public health officer, or I could remain in the USPHS. But what I would come to learn about organizations, families, and children—and what I needed to know about why people do what they do—moved me to commit myself to addressing a huge problem in my small way. Also, I saw the social justice implications in our failure to provide a good education—the only road to mainstream opportunity— for these children. I believed that societal institutions could, and indeed had a responsibility, to do so.

Through working with people in need at Hospitality House, I became acutely aware of a pervasive "failure is your own fault" mentality in our society. The individual was responsible; society had no responsibility. The implication was that anyone who was not able to survive and thrive without help either was not smart enough or did not work hard enough. Even the poor, themselves, often believed that their plight was entirely their own fault. They experienced a high level of scorn from service providers and other mainstream people regularly, contributing to their low self respect and decreasing hope. These dispositions did not and could not help them help themselves. And while the importance of self help was at the core of my family and cultural experience, I was also raised with the belief that we—all members of society—should help one another.

Thus, I chose to study public health with a focus on the responsibility of the individual to the society and the responsibility of the society and it's institutions to the individual. It was during this study that a working model which positioned society–family–child interactions as powerful determinants of individual behavior began to emerge. Prompted by my interest in environmental ecology, in my term paper for a child and family course I proposed that the school was a critical intervention site within the spectrum of experiences children need to mature and perform adequately in life. I argued that the school was strategically located in everyone's developmental pathway, that education was a positively valued activity, and that schools had more adult growth mediators than any other institution. As a result of all of these factors, I argued, the school was in a position to reinforce good preparation for learning and life and to compensate for poor preparation.

Later on, I realized that I had underestimated the complexity of the obstacles preventing schools from acting as I proposed. Good preparation for school required good development before and during school, but development does not have a central, highly valued place in the education enterprise.

Early in my year at the school of public health, 1963–1964, I decided that one of the useful ways I could position myself in medicine was to become a psychiatrist. At the 1964 University of Michigan graduation, President Lyndon Banes Johnson spoke about creating the "Great Society." He charged us graduates to use our knowledge and skills to "do something" for the poor and for the country. President Kennedy had been assassinated during that school year, and Civil Rights tensions were mounting. "Do something" reverberated strongly in my head and my heart as President Johnson's helicopter took off from the graduation site in a dramatic cloud of dust. But what should I do? This was my state of mind as I entered my psychiatry training.

My training in adult psychiatry at the Yale University Department of Psychiatry led to training in child and adolescent development and psychiatry at the Yale Child Study Center (YCSC). During my training in adult psychiatry, I learned that many adult behavioral problems were related to family, school, and community problems from the patient's childhood. I also noted that psychiatry often located the cause of behavioral problems in the individual, and at most, the family. Community, history, and cultural factors were very rarely discussed. My training in child and adolescent psychiatry—and, more importantly, my life experiences—deepened my belief that, in order to understand and prevent difficult, sometimes pathological, psychological disorders, it was important to look beyond the individual.

I returned to the USPHS and was assigned to the National Institute of Mental Health (NIMH) in Washington, D.C., in 1967. I was greatly dissatisfied that the brief flurry of professional interest in social psychiatry and related demonstration studies generated by urban unrest was declining rapidly. The new push was for "more rigorous" experimental research design studies, which were seen as being more scientific. Maybe so, but were the findings as useful and could they inform and guide interventions as well as hands-on, field or action-based observations and qualitative or ethnographic studies supported by experiments?

The limits of the push for rigor were apparent in one particular big, expensive, quasi-experimental research-design study that was being planned. Researchers were to study five American cities that experienced riots as a result of racial discontent and compare them to five American cities that did not experience riots (the control group). Ironically, before they could get the study off the ground, riots erupted in the control group cities. I suggested that such a study was like trying to measure the impact of waving a fan over a feather in a wind tunnel; the methodology and tools being used were inadequate. If there was any discussion about the limits of the research design at NIMH, I was not in the room.

I considered several things when I asked myself why and how the NIMH study was flawed. I reasoned that, in order to understand complex individual and group behaviors and events, it is necessary to consider the interaction of at least five major influences: human nature, culture, history, individual and group experiences, and internal mind and external life situations. This is not easy to do in a precise and quantifiable way; indeed, it's nearly impossible.

Quantification is very important in the academic research community. Thus, powerful behavioral influences were not being considered because they were not quantifiable. The largely socio-economic factors the researchers were considering in the NIMH study could not explain the complex situation or provide insight for effective intervention. There had to be another way.

When the late Albert Solnit, then the director of the YCSC, invited me to return and direct an intervention program in schools, I leapt at the chance. I chose to return to Yale because, having trained there, I knew that the psychiatry program was eclectic. Highly regarded senior faculty were doing exciting work in the social, child development, psychological, psychoanalytic, biological, community, and preventive areas. I sensed that working in schools was going to take me beyond individual factors, and at Yale, I would be allowed to find my way and not be locked into traditional ways of doing research.

Also, the Yale Child Study Center leadership group was concerned about the tendency of behavioral scientists to impose established research and practice methods—and labels—on people and situations where their use was not appropriate or helpful. I was being asked to find a more appropriate and effective way to use mental health principles to serve children who were not ill but who were not succeeding as well as possible in school and in life. The late Bill Kessen, a distinguished psychologist, and others thoroughly reviewed our goals and our research plan, and we all concluded that an exploratory demonstration model would be more useful than a quasi-experimental, quantitative approach.

Our project was a joint effort between the New Haven Public School System (NHPSS) and our team from the Yale Child Study Center (YCSC). The pilot was in two of the lowest achieving—academically, socially, and behaviorally—elementary schools within the system. Our strategy was to live in these two schools and learn about schooling. Then, with the input of all the participants, we would improve schooling locally and then beyond.

Because this was not a common way of working, there was little useful literature to guide our work. Our team used our personal experiences and professional training as a framework for identifying the critical underlying problems of the school and for fashioning and implementing an effective intervention method. While I was not fully aware of what I was doing at the time, the intervention model we used was the diagnostic and treatment approach from medicine. The knowledge and skills gained from life experience and professional training informed our diagnostic efforts and treatment/intervention approaches. The "patient" was the dysfunctional system(s)—including classroom and building practices, policymakers, and practice leaders at every level.

The initial intervention research had to be qualitative—demonstration, observation, description, assessment, and modification aimed at achieving goals. We were applying sound theory, principles, and some empirical evidence to practice. But because it was not like traditional work in education and the behavioral sciences, there was much confusion, doubt, and skepticism about our methods.

A colleague who came to Yale from elsewhere told me that, when she heard about what we were doing, she imagined that I was some kind of "guru-freak"—a "nice man, quietly charismatic, but out there." Another preventive psychiatrist asked me, "But *who* is your patient?!" We lost our initial funding after 5 years because the supporting foundation asked psychiatrists to assess our chance for success and were told that the approach could not work because the students needed one-to-one psychiatric care. During our third project year, a reporter for *Connecticut Magazine* observed the school for a week and acknowledged that it was well-functioning and that the participants were thriving, but said he couldn't write a story because he could not understand how the outcomes came about.

Oddly, and not so oddly, my mother understood. She was a bit worried about "my son the doctor" working first in psychiatry and then in schools. On a trip home she asked me what I did in the schools, and I described how we helped change the climate and culture of the schools so that the adults could interact with the students and provide them with experiences that would help them grow up in such a way that they would be motivated to learn. The examples I gave were much like the interactions and experiences she and my dad had shared with me and my siblings. She looked at me in disbelief and said, "But that's common sense!" As I was recovering from that shot, she followed with, "And they pay you for that?!"

I agree with my mother: Good childhood experiences are the foundation for good learning and good development. This should be common sense. But this point of view was in the minority for a long time— and probably still is, even now. I also had a sense that the absence of such experiences was a major reason that my three childhood friends—and many children like them—did not do well in school and in life.

Over the first 15 years of our School Development Program (SDP) intervention model, we facilitated improved development, behavior, and academic learning in our pilot project schools and in about a dozen field-test schools in various parts of the country. The model was then disseminated widely. Over the 40-year life of the program, it has been used in over 1,000 schools in more than 80 school districts in 26 states and several Caribbean and European countries. We have been able to observe and sometimes measure the conditions that facilitate desired outcomes and those that limit and prevent, both of which have proven useful for suggesting ways that policies and practices can be changed and designed to greatly improve our system(s) of education on a large scale.

Planning and Start-Up

When we were planning the YCSC project in 1967, Al Solnit asked me whether I would favor a pilot project involving one school that was de facto racially segregated and one where busing was used to bring about integration or one involving two schools that were both de facto segregated. I chose the latter. I had not yet identified underdevelopment and the absence of ability to promote development in school as the underlying problem, but having lived with one foot in an integrated school and the other in an African American primary social network, I suspected that it was the vitality and sense of inclusion in the latter that was more important to development. My academic success and that of my siblings was due to the powerful presence of our family and our connection to the racially integrated school that made the critical school learning dynamic possible for us. Our friends who did not have such connections did not fare as well.

This is not to say that I was or am opposed to school integration. The national decision to end school segregation helped to break the powerful symbol of racial inferiority that was used to deny Blacks equal opportunity in all aspects of American life. In general I believed that school integration should proceed where possible, but I knew from experience that school integration did not ensure equal opportunity for Black students. I was concerned that, in our project, the integration effort might consume the energy needed to explore the equal opportunity question.

I had been in the predominantly White Washington School since kindergarten when, in my 5th-grade year, the fifth and sixth grades at the predominantly Black Columbus School were closed and the students were sent to Washington School. There were no in-school orientations, plans, or introductions that we students knew about. Integration just happened. Classroom conditions were polite but awkward and tense. During a classroom exercise in which we were working in small groups planning skits, one of the new Black male students touched one of the new Black female students. She was offended and responded, "Get your hands off me, Nigger!" A sudden hush fell on the room, and my Black and White classmates looked at me.

I was a leader, but that was probably only part of the reason for this reaction. I had been a classmate and friend of most of the White students at Washington School for the previous 5 years. My older sister had been a much loved teacher of the Black students at Columbus School. These relationships formed the basis of trust from both sides, and my authority. I was able to point out that "we don't use *that word* [not yet called the N word] in this school." My classmate apologized and we went back to work as if nothing had happened.

I suspect that most of our teachers—all White—whether they agreed with the merging of students from Washington and Columbus Schools or not, simply wanted to do their job and wanted to be fair. In that same class, as a class exercise, we selected class officers every week. I pointed out that my White friends repeatedly selected other "old students" and never any of the "new students," and that changed immediately. Concerned about what my White teacher thought about my stance, I looked back where she sat knitting and listening. She gave me a wink of approval.

To the surprise of my sister, even some of her former students from Columbus who she considered to have high academic potential did not do well in the new setting. That summer, I participated in a Baptist Church Sunday school class at Columbus School with my Black classmates from Washington school. I either underestimated the competition or took my vacation too seriously, because I received the second-lowest test score in the class—to the surprise of all. With more training, my understanding of what happed was that my very able classmates did well in an environment in which they experienced a sense of belonging and where they felt wanted and valued and not so well when they didn't feel so or were not sure.

These incidents suggest that the major underlying problem is not one of student ability or potential, and not one of unwillingness on the part of school staff to help all their students, but mainly the absence of knowledge, skills, structures, and processes that would enable staff, parents, and students to create an inclusive school culture that promotes good development and learning among all students. During my adult psychiatry training, I began to get an idea of what might help create these conditions.

As a part of my training, I worked in a milieu therapy setting. I was struck by how the need to belong in the group promoted positive relationships and responsible behavior. Such achievement was a part of what it meant to be successful and to improve one's mental health and functioning. On reflection, as a child I often avoided problem behaviors in order to be respected by people in my family, church, and community—even when the problem behavior might have been pleasurable. I also wanted to experience the signs and symbols of belonging. One Easter Sunday, decorated eggs were given to the children in my church, but there weren't going to be enough eggs to go around. Ms. Johnson pulled me out of line because she knew that my parents would have an Easter egg hunt for us at home. She did the right thing and even explained the reason for her action to me, but my 6-year-old heart ached. I wanted my egg with everybody else; I wanted to participate, to belong.

Reflecting on such experiences has helped me understand the power of the human need to belong in a group and the need to be recognized and rewarded by fellow members for efforts that meet group approval. This explains why my childhood friends, and others like them, didn't do well in school, but I still had a lot to learn about why the school did not do well with them. The first- and second-year planning and implementation of our project began to supply such understanding.

While the question about our focus—racial integration or creating a supportive setting—was informed largely by my life experience, our decisions about staffing and about how we would work were informed largely by knowledge from our behavioral science training and the way we envisioned our tasks. The NHPSS had responsibility for the instructional program, and our YCSC team had responsibility for providing support services and guiding innovation. Thus, our YCSC team was made up of a psychiatrist, two social workers, a special education teacher, a research and evaluation psychologist, and a helping teacher/log keeper. We purposefully selected disciplines that were commonly found in schools. In this way future innovations might require existing people to work differently, but not require extraordinary new costs. Once the schools stabilized, I would move back from front-line involvement because the high-cost services of a psychiatrist would not be needed or affordable in most settings.

Unwittingly, separating relationship, behavioral, and instructional issues as we did quickly led us to one of the central problems in education: *a very strong focus on curriculum, instruction, and assessment without an adequate focus on relationships and development.* The NHPSS had hired a group of young educators who used an open-classroom instructional approach. Others used a traditional instructional approach. Our SDP staff wanted to focus on preparation for students and parents in a way that could lead to positive interactions and good relationships among and between students, staff, and parents. We acquiesced to learning the new open-classroom instructional approach. Because of the focus on instruction without an equal focus on organization and management, leadership was not clear, and there was no mechanism for role clarification, planning, goal setting, developing problem-solving and achievement strategies, and the many other things needed to get a new program off the ground. This led to ineffective communication, confusion, and rancor.

As a result, on opening day the school exploded! Things were out of control throughout the first month. Students and staff were acting out in troublesome ways. Parents were angry, and some confronted our team and the school leadership; others simply withdrew, disappointed. In turn, there was staff frustration and anger about the lack of parental support. In the absence or effective leadership, decisions were made by factions and cliques through power and coercion, further increasing the tensions.

Instead of listening and learning, we had to get directly involved in order to survive. We learned more as participant observers than we ever could have as "objective" observers and/or researchers acting from an implementation protocol. Using the one-on-one medical model treatment approach, our support staff—social workers, special education teacher, helping teacher, and others—couldn't handle the many referrals for services. We quickly learned that mandates for change and lectures about child development did not help very much. Some of the staff who liked what they heard could not apply it in the classroom. Teachers and administrators who came in with high hopes in the beginning ended up losing hope, burned out, and began to leave.

During the first month—due to a parental and community mandate to either get it right or get out—we created a governance and management team, still the most important program element, that was representative of all the school stakeholders: teachers, administrators, and professional support staff (social worker, psychologist, etc.); non-professional support staff; and parents. This team, with the support of our YCSC-SDP team, had the task of righting our badly listing, all but sunken, ship. The idea was that turning over ownership and responsibility to the major stakeholders in the school, while providing them with access to our knowledge and skills about children and systems, would promote effective problem solving.

We addressed the most pressing problems first and made progress on a couple occasions, including adding eight program components during the first year. But too much damage had been done. In a school climate where people don't know, trust, or like one another, the smallest student or staff problem can and did lead to disruptions that caused recovery efforts to fail. It had become clear by then that we couldn't turn things around without a major conceptual and intervention change. Toward the end of the first school year, I held separate half-day talks with two key parent leaders, sharing my reasons for being there, including my personal experiences and my dreams and hopes for their children. I promised that we would turn bad into good (back when bad meant bad and good meant good) in a second year. They called on the other parents to give us another year.

And while the first year was a very powerful learning experience, it was hurtful to all involved—staff, students, and parents. Our recovery effort led us to another major insight: *the need to focus on the building as a system and as the target of intervention.* The dysfunctional system was as much or more the problem than were the individual students, staff, volunteers, and parents. This was a unique perspective at the time.

Survival and Continued Learning

I remember a conversation with our chief social worker toward the end of the first year in which we agreed that we would have to focus first and foremost on the school as a system. Trying to address individual student and family problems had not been very useful. In the first year,

60 percent of the social work time had gone to five students and their families, and there were few results to show for the time. Also, "tons" of volunteers and groups were in the schools trying to be helpful. The many individual program parts and people were moving and/or being propelled without sufficient thought about how learning would take place and about planning and system orchestration.

Once we had time to really think about what happened during that first year, our focus on the system was supported. We realized that there were really no "bad guys." Everybody in the two pilot schools—parents, professional and non-professional support staff, and students—were failing but wanted to succeed. The troublesome behavior they displayed was a reaction to failure, and the failure was due to the absence of structures and processes that made success possible.

Recovery was difficult; every step of the way, our work was informed by our diagnostic and treatment perspective from medicine, our public health ecology or interaction-based perspective, knowledge of child and adult development and functioning, and observations in practice. These were conveyed to our colleagues—parents and staff, eventually students—and they used them to solve authentic, real-world problems. This led to a school culture that promoted adequate to high levels of development and learning among students, staff, and parents.

We used the summer before the second year to enable the staff and parents to get to know one another and to think about, refine, and use the emerging SDP model. First, we wanted to understand how students develop and how their development is related to learning. Second, we wanted to create the school environment, climate, and/or culture needed to help the adults interact well with the students and help the students develop. We used a refined version of the nine-element process model we put together in the first year.

The nine elements are the *school planning and management team,* the *student and staff support team,* the *parent team, no-fault problem solving, consensus decision-making, collaboration,* development of a *comprehensive school plan,* provision of *staff development,* and *assessment and modification* as needed. I won't go into the details of the process model here, but I'd like to share an example of how the nine elements can come together to improve school culture and community.

An 8-year-old transfer student met his new teacher for the first time just inside the door of the classroom. He kicked her in the leg, turned, and ran out. The principal asked our *student and staff support team* to help.

We learned that the student had been transferred over the weekend from a small, tight-knit community in rural North Carolina by an aunt. The student had been dropped off at school on Monday morning as she continued on to work. The teacher had received three transfers the week before, and this latest one frustrated her. As a result, she unintentionally conveyed rejection to the child. His home and community social and emotional support system had been abruptly removed, and he was in a strange town, at a strange school, about to interact with students he didn't know and with a teacher who did not appear to want him. His immature social-psycho-emotional defensive and adaptive capacities couldn't contain his anxiety, and he kicked and ran—reasonably understandable and healthy 8-year-old behavior.

When the behavior was understood as underdevelopment, or immaturity, and the absence of a child-friendly transfer support process in the school—rather than as an example of "another bad kid"—the teacher's anger turned to a desire to help. The teacher and her colleagues suggested procedures and activities that could help the child feel wanted and comfortable, and these were put into place immediately.

The incident was reported to the *school planning and management team,* and at their suggestion, became a full *staff development* activity. The *parent team* was informed and also made suggestions. This systematic *assessment* led to a useful *modification* to the *comprehensive school plan:* the creation of a regular transfer or new student procedure. In this process there was *no-fault problem solving.* The new student procedure was agreed on through *consensus,* informed by child development knowledge, and the staff and parents worked *collaboratively* to overcome what had been a serious ongoing problem because of the high mobility of students in low-income communities. The resulting decrease in tension producing incidents contributed to the promotion of a positive school climate and culture.

All nine elements of the SDP framework, operating systematically, helped the staff pull together people, knowledge, and skills in a coordinated, orchestrated, efficient, effective, growth producing way. The effort was synchronous and synergistic.

Many people have asked me how and why the framework and process, or tool, works. *It works because, when the tool is used to solve a problem or advance a school plan, the staff and parents have a sense of efficacy and competence.* They learn and act effectively from thinking, working, and reflecting together and individually—they are empowered. Rewarding practice and social and psycho-emotional outcomes motivate them to strive to be even more successful.

At the end of the "kick and run" incident, I joked to the teachers and administrators, "That was a situation of fight-*and*-flight rather than fight-*or*-flight." They looked at me like I was speaking a foreign language. They did not know what I was talking about. Almost every first-year social and behavioral science student would have understood my meaning. The fight–or-flight reaction is a basic and well-known response to stress. There may be more social and behavioral scientists per population in New Haven than anywhere in the world, but these New Haven teachers were out there on the front line without having received this basic knowledge. It was at this moment that I had my great epiphany: *Teachers are not being adequately prepared to teach children—their primary mission.* They are not being given the yeast needed to bake the bread—they are not shown how to apply child development knowledge and skills to their practice.

In 1968, many preparatory programs didn't even require child development courses. And while almost all require them now, most do not help teachers learn how to create a positive school environment and to intentionally integrate development, curriculum, instruction, and assessment in the service of good learning and desirable behavior.

School people can't be expected to connect most students to learning if they themselves only have "book and discussion" knowledge about child development, behavior, and learning and little to no knowledge about how to create the climate and/or culture in practice needed to promote development and learning. Equally troublesome, most parents and the public believe that school people are being adequately prepared and many teacher educators believe that they are adequately preparing them. Indeed, I had assumed that teachers and administrators knew more about the development and learning connection than was apparent.

But many teachers and administrators, particularly in settings where the children come to school underdeveloped, know that they were not adequately prepared. Fifty percent of new teachers leave after their first 5 years, and one of their biggest reasons for leaving is that there is no way for them to influence their conditions of practice. And even if there were ways for them to do so, many would not be prepared to do so. The SDP framework is designed to engage all the stakeholders in creating effective living and learning conditions in "our school."

After the meeting about the "kick and run" incident was over, I stayed in that empty room, stunned, thinking about how unfair this lack of knowledge and skills really was, and how different my own preparation for working with children was to the teachers.' When I was doing play therapy with a hyperactive 8-year-old girl, she threatened to throw paint on me. As soon as possible, I went to my supervisor and told him the story. He smiled and said, "She likes you." I thought to myself that, if so, she has a very strange way of showing it! He explained that she did not know how to play and suggested that the next time she threatened me; I should tell her that, if she threw the paint, I would be so angry that I would not want to play with her. I couldn't imagine how that would stop "the wild child," the name we trainees had privately given her. In self defense, the next time she threatened I used his advice. She slowly put the paint can down, and I gave her playing lessons; we agreed on a few rules, also.

I am not suggesting that teachers need the same training that psychiatrists receive, but they do need to know more about what the inner life of a child is about, how children cope with and respond to the daily challenges of school life, with and without adequate preparation to do so, and how teachers can provide the children with activities and interactions that will help them develop, learn, and grow.

The lack of acceptance of the evidence that the understanding and application of child and adolescent development in practice is the foundation for academic learning is probably the reason that a graduate student in Wisconsin asked to be excused from the child development course because "I'm a principal and I won't need it."

Our SDP framework was used to address all that went on in the schools. As the behavior problems declined, it was possible to focus more on the social and academic program needs identified through regular assessments. After 5 years the schools were greatly improved, but the test scores had not gone up significantly. It was at this point that the foundation supporting our work consulted psychiatrists who said that our approach could not be successful because psychotherapy was needed.

During a phase-out year, a NHPSS social worker began to serve the schools and to remove students for treatment. A group of teachers marched into the principal's office and demanded that he not allow the social worker back in the school. They had gained skills and now viewed problem behaviors as opportunities to help their students grow; as a result, the teachers expected the school to provide useful consultation for them to deal with the problem, not to remove the student. The parents were now delighted with the schools. While we had to obtain another funding source to do so, we survived again, this time because of the outcomes and not on a promise.

But why were the test scores not going up? One day, when the lobby of one of the schools was being used as a polling place for an election, the probable cause hit me. When I was 9 or 10 years old, I remember visiting my mother while she was serving as an election poll worker. I actually went in and pulled the lever for her vote, illegal of course, but a moment of extraordinary triumph; a precious memory. Lev Vygotsky emphasized the daily life of the child as the platform of culture acquisition, the source of attitudes, values, self expression, and problem-solving ways. It was the supportive experiences in my daily life—not race, class, or significantly greater intelligence—that led to a more rewarding school and adult life for me as opposed to my three friends.

"Yes!" I realized. Mainstream children gain the disposition and skills needed to be successful in school by growing up in environments that provide them with such a disposition and skills. With content based on the aspirations the parents had for their children, we designed an activity entitled the "Social Skills Curriculum for Inner City Children" (SSCICC). It became a component of our comprehensive school plan and was funded by the Minority Center of NIMH.

The SDP pilot schools designed four activity units that encouraged parent, staff, and student interactions that would better prepare the students for success in school and in life: politics and government, business and economics, health and nutrition, and spiritual and leisure time. The teaching and learning of basic academic knowledge and skills, social-interactive skills, an appreciation of the arts and athletics, and related knowledge and skills were integrated and embedded in the unit activities. The academic work included reading, writing, mathematics, social studies, science, history, drama, and music. The adults related the content and activities to the developmental pathways that were important to school and life success—social-interactive, psycho-emotional, moral-ethical, physical, linguistic, cognitive, and academic development—and intentionally mediated student acquisition of knowledge and skills in these pathways.

In the dance performance that was a part of the politics and government unit, the staff was surprised to discover that some students who did not do well academically had remarkable personal presence and interacted well with the mayor and other dignitaries in attendance. One teacher noted that her students enjoyed the presentation by a doctor during a health and nutrition unit activity, but didn't really understand much of what he said until she helped them use the information in more concrete classroom activities. She speculated that the "do this, don't do this" kind of talks given by fireman, policeman, and other one-time visitors probably are of limited value without such follow-up.

These activities paralleled the "exposure and participation" in mainstream activities that had been so important in my own development and that play a major role in how most mainstream students are prepared at home. Again, and most important, the school staff embedded academic content in meaningful simulated mainstream activities that provided meaningful exposure and participation experiences, while promoting development and motivating academic learning.

I expected the SSCICC approach to work, but even I was surprised by the magnitude of its positive impact on everybody. The experience energized and benefited everybody in the setting. It gave them self-esteem, hope, a sense of purpose, and more. When students learned about local government, it increased their interest in and knowledge about national government. Some of the parents who got involved in the politics and government unit activities registered and voted in the regular election for the first time in their lives. This gave teachers a much more encouraging view of the potential of their students.

The test scores soared.

Dissemination, Resistance, and Inertia

We had shown that the problem was not the students, staff, or parents but *the building as a system,* and that the system could be fixed. That was obvious, right? All we had to do at this point was to help others do the same, first locally and then nationally, demonstration after demonstration.

Not so fast; there was resistance and inertia to contend with. There had been resistance to change in our pilot schools, but as the process yielded good outcomes, most people "bought in" or left. We attributed the resistance largely to human nature; it's difficult to change established habits without strong motivation. But we would learn that the causes of resistance were deeper, more varied, and more pervasive than we first thought.

The superintendent arranged two presentations of our work and outcomes, and they were very well received, but only two other schools in New Haven were interested in using the process. The principal of one is now the current NHPSS superintendent and is supporting an SDP implementation renewal.

The other principal headed a school 1 mile down the street in the same socioeconomic level neighborhood. He prepared me for disappointment by pointing out that we would not have the same success in his school as in our pilot schools. When questioned, he said that while the students in our pilot schools were poor, his students were poor *and* from a housing project. I countered that the students from one of our pilot schools were also from a housing project. He pointed out that our students were from a two-story project complex and his were from a high-rise and told us that there was research showing that the latter fared worse.

The way we do and transmit research findings is a part of the problem. Our nation spends billions of dollars on what I call "bits and pieces" social problem research. Most consumers don't have the knowledge base or integrative framework needed to pull it together as a useful whole, and insight. Without a framework or the complementary knowledge (human nature, history, culture, experience, and situation) needed to understand the data, some findings can do as much or more harm than good. What this principal had learned was harmful.

To the principal's credit he was cooperative and there was impressive improvement. Reporting on the progress to the superintendent he mentioned a puzzling experience. On the day that the male faculty members, as a school climate–improvement activity, prepared an in-school breakfast for the women, there was a good feeling in the building all day long. As an afterthought he mentioned, with a tone of surprise, that there was not a student fight that entire day. He didn't get the positive climate–development–behavior and learning connection.

A year later, on my second visit to a field-test school, a young African American teacher told his colleagues how he became a believer in the SDP process. The first time he heard me describe the social skills activity, or SSCICC, he privately rejected the idea as a violation of the students' culture. Later he and other teachers took a busload of students to meet people from the local community college who had adopted his class and planned to tutor them. It was a bucolic campus that had a stream running through it with geese and ducks peacefully floating along. A bridge over the stream separated the arriving class and their smiling hosts on the other side.

Two of the young boys jumped off the bus, and in glee picked up rocks and began to throw them at the birds. Amid the honking and squawking, and the then horrified look on the faces of the hosts, the teacher ordered all back on the bus. He developed a relationship unit that enabled them to return, manage the experience well, and benefit from the tutoring and other interactions. Bad boys? No, just underdeveloped in the social-interactive area. He realized that rather than violating their culture, the knowledge and skills learned gave them an option other than being locked outside the societal mainstream.

We implemented the model in the field-test phase in various parts of the country and found that where there was acceptance of the ideas, or "buy in," and reasonable competence, it worked. But there was significant resistance to the ideas everywhere. *It began to appear that the problem was more than simply human nature; a reluctance to change.*

Teacher comments about their experience with implementing the SDP process suggested reasons for the depth, pervasiveness, and tenacity of the inertia and resistance. For some, it was largely a problem of change. But for most the SDP focus on helping students grow and develop took them out of their comfort zone. Their traditional beliefs and ways of thinking and doing things were no longer being praised or rewarded. Others said that the notion that all students could perform at a high level was new and challenging. They were pointing to a very deep and powerful cultural mindset—reflected in our traditional education beliefs and practices—which say that limited student capacity, not the quality of schooling, is the problem; that some can learn and some can't.

This traditional understanding of how and why children learn has led to a mechanistic model of adult-centered, often authoritarian teaching and passive student learning, with progress standards and assessments that are narrowly focused on test scores. Little attention is given to the developmental capacities and knowledge that students need to acquire and use to succeed in life.

There is now evidence that the interaction between the child and his or her environment, particularly key caretakers, greatly influences brain development and functioning—that nature is in large part nurture. (This is not to say that there are not differences in ability levels, but this is probably due more to developmental experiences than to race, region, or socio-economic class.) This tells us that teachers and administrators should support the creation of in-school cultures that support children's development. Also, some believe that it is the student's will that determines behavior and achievement. This is, in part, true, but a student's will is in large part a developmental outcome.

Thus, our SDP approach flew in the face of entrenched cultural beliefs and practices that had been institutionalized and transmitted from one generation to the next. While pondering whether it was possible to move Mt. Everest, I heard about the Danish system of education, which was built on family, community, school, and developmental interaction principles that were similar to our SDP approach. The Danish principles were put forth by a 19th-century philosopher, N.F.S. Grundtvig. Denmark has been ranked among the top five countries in the world in economic competitiveness repeatedly, and their system of schooling is heavily credited for their success.

Before going to observe Danish system, I interviewed a 16-year-old Danish exchange student in a middle-income, racially integrated American school. He spoke warmly about the supportive relationships he experienced in his Danish school and described how the teachers treated the students like their own children and how this motivated him to work hard and behave well so as not to disappoint them, his family, or himself. He described the work as demanding but fun and peer relationships as relaxed and rewarding.

The next hour I spoke with his American classmates. Most felt that some of their teachers were caring and supportive, but too many were not. They complained that some teachers didn't know their names, gave preferential treatment to the best academic students, and were not available to them beyond the narrow academic school day. "They beat us out the door at the end of the day." They argued with one another about whether it was the teachers' fault or the students' fault. The call for personal responsibility was admirable, but the question of fault was irrelevant. What was important and tragic was that the school culture they described was harmful to the development and growth of the students, staff, and school as a community.

The Danish system is designed so that there is a close and seamless tie between home and school and a continuity of support for development from birth to maturity. A parent–teacher group keeps the community connected to the school. And a single teacher moves with a class across the years, sometimes with one change half way. Other teachers work with the class teacher to provide traditional academic subjects as well as a broad spectrum of activities the students need to develop fully—art, music, physical education, home economics, and more. The school principal is selected for administrative training after demonstrating, as a teacher, his or her ability to promote the kind of school culture that supports student development. A teacher with knowledge of child development and behaviors supports other teachers as needed.

I asked how they handled ineffective teachers. My host found the explanation difficult to put in writing, but after a long delay she called. She explained that they don't have many ineffective teachers in the Danish system because the teacher's union selects and makes hiring recommendations to the local government authority, makes arrangements to provide foundering new teachers with help, and negotiates their release when it is clear they can't perform adequately. Surely, I insisted, there must be some who are protected by nepotism, favoritism, and other human frailties? The answer was, "They would not select or tolerate poor performance because they would not want to hurt the children." That's different!

My visit to Denmark strongly suggested to me that our SDP was pushing in the right direction with our focus on child development as a way to prevent problem behaviors and to promote preparation for life, as opposed to the traditional focus on academic achievement deficits and behavior problems, with attempted control through punishment. It also suggested, again, that our education problem is lodged least in the students and their families and most in our system of schooling.

From my initial realization that teachers and administrators were not being given the support and information they needed to help students achieve school success, I felt that the critical place to intervene would be in our teacher and administrator preparatory institutions. Teachers and administrators are more likely to support student development and integrate developmental principles into their curriculum and instruction when doing so is a part of their professional identity, established for most between 18–25 years of age. Thus, we designed our dissemination phase as collaboration between our SDP, several schools of education, and several school districts. The goal was to have pre-service students and some pre-service teachers supporting them in the field begin to help their university-based colleagues appreciate the power of a developmental perspective. We also worked with one social service agency, almost all social workers, and we continued some direct work with schools and districts. In time, the university units and social service organization that worked with us were able to serve schools and districts with minimum, and then no, SDP staff presence.

We worked anywhere possible but tried to work in two or more schools in the same area to increase our chance of being successful with one so as to decrease resistance in the others. We then worked to create clusters of successful schools as a strategy for eventually getting "buy in" throughout the districts. We noticed, however, that regardless of the intervention arrangements, about one-third of the schools improved dramatically, about one-third improved modestly, and about one-third did not improve. We also noticed that success paralleled the degree of "buy in" and quality of the implementation effort.

It did not appear that the performance difference was due to significantly different staff competence levels. And only a few greatly improved schools could sustain their gains because of the leadership turnover. Because broad "buy in" didn't exist, a new superintendent who did not like the SDP focus could simply eliminate or slowly destroy outcomes that took five years to achieve.

When one SDP school went from being the lowest-achieving school to the highest, the superintendent decided that they must be cheating. With great media fanfare and under central office management, the students had to take the state test over again. When the students did even better the second time there was almost no media coverage. But by removing the principal and making a few other questionable personnel changes, the school was plunged back to its underperforming status within a year.

The summer after the plunge, at the airport I bumped into the school science teacher, a talented young African American woman who loved teaching and wanted to stay in education. She was on her way to accept a job with a pharmaceutical company because her joy in teaching was gone. In another case, a principal was moved who supported the SDP, and the staff requested a similar leader. The request was granted and that low-income school continued to rival suburban schools until personnel changes finally weakened its success.

Faced with repeated problems of resistance, inertia, and turnover, we stopped trying to increase the number of schools and districts we worked with and focused on trying to prevent negative outcomes by promoting system-wide leadership support for our SDP approach. We had noted that when district leadership strongly sanctioned the use of our program principles, school "buy in" was greater and outcomes were better. So we worked to get strong support from the school board, superintendent, union, buildings, and parents.

To get the broadest and deepest level of support for our application of child and adolescent development principles possible, we began a five–district, systemwide project in 1998. All the schools produced good to remarkable outcomes by 2005. In one district, the academic achievement proficiency gap between more-affluent-than-usual White students and poor Black students was all but closed by fifth grade, even as White achievement improved and the Black poverty level increased slightly over the period.

While there was less resistance to the approach in these five districts, turnover due to personal, political, and relationship reasons was still too high to make it possible for schools and districts to build on gains and continue to grow. Also, while the school of education and social work people who collaborated with our SDP school districts sometimes made dramatic academic and behavioral improvements, the changes in their own institutions were minimal, even when some wanted to change, and the future teachers in their courses spoke glowingly of the benefit of creating a supportive school culture and integrating developmental principles with curriculum, instruction, and assessment activities.

Our work suggests that the absence of such knowledge and skills when teachers and administrators enter practice contributes heavily to all school problems, particularly the turnover of new teacher problem.

After our five-district project, we had to concede that theory, research, and demonstrations can't overcome the effects of deep-seated, long-standing, entrenched traditional education policies and practices. We continue to work with schools, districts, schools of education, and social service people, but it is our impression that only focused policy and practice changes, facilitated at every level of government and supported with public and private advocacy, can be powerful enough to overcome the ill effects of an almost exclusive focus on curriculum, instruction, and assessment and minimal or marginal attention to engendering the sort of whole-child development that prepares our students for participation in school and in life.

Toward a World-Class System of Education

There is much to suggest that high-quality school organization, management, and teaching is the key to improving American education. Much good work has been done to promote such outcomes over the last 20 to 25 years—particularly learning communities, a very useful step. But even these efforts do not adequately take into account the centrality and foundational function of child and adolescent development. My colleague Linda Darling-Hammond has compared development to the trunk of a tree, and academic learning and preparation for life as the branches and all else that grow out from that trunk. I concur and encouraged such thinking.

I would add that, like the tree, good growth—and in this metaphor, development and academic learning—requires adequate nourishment. Our SDP work, and that of others, even other nations, as seen in the Danish example, demonstrates that a good school culture can provide much of the nourishment needed to promote high-level development and academic learning among all—when school staff have the tools to create such a culture.

There is growing evidence that student underdevelopment and staff underpreparation to support development in school is a major cause of student and staff underachievement. But even now, much of the focus and fuss around school improvement is about education delivery systems— public, private, vouchers, charters, others—and curriculum, instruction and assessment methods.

My 40 years of work suggests that, no matter what the delivery system or instructional focus, we need a very deep pool of educators who understand student development, how it's related to academic learning and preparation for life, and how to use the related knowledge and skills in practice. To be most effective, such preparation should take place while teachers' professional identity is being established during pre-service study; but it also can occur through in-service training aimed at modifying inadequate traditional practice, and it can be reinforced through the integration of development and academic teaching and learning.

At best the patchwork of new interventions that have sprouted over the last 25 years—even when effective—can only serve a small percentage of our students. Many have not proven effective, and have not been the source of significant new insights. Nationwide school improvement can only come about when most of our public school workforce, supported by community and policy changes, can adequately support student development and academic learning.

Most traditional preparatory institutions do not currently provide teacher and administrator candidates with the needed tools, but with change, they could and should do so. Preparatory institutions and districts will need hands on help to be able to prepare pre- and in-service teachers to integrate child and adolescent development principles with curriculum, instruction, and assessment in order to promote student learning and preparation for life. And that can be done.

But many smart people have given up on the schools of education. We can't. As long as thousands of young people who want to be successful teachers pour though these programs and into our schools—and eventually out of education because they were not adequately prepared—we cannot hope to have a world class education system. I'm reminded of what the famous Depression-era bank robber Willie Sutton said when asked why he robbed banks: "'Cause that's where the money is." The same goes for schools of education and other teacher preparatory programs: "That's where the teachers and administrators are."

Education, all aspects, like 19th-century medicine, is plagued with "solutions." The creation of best practice knowledge bases; practice centered research that informed teaching, the accreditation of medical schools and the certification of medical practitioners helped to improve the discipline. Doing the same with teacher and administrator preparatory and certification programs could achieve the same.

State and national funding incentives for programs that have a proven track record of preparing pre- and in-service teachers to meet their students' educational and developmental needs can have a significant impact. Policy changes at the national, state, and local levels to make practice changes possible at every level will also be needed. But I offer an important caveat here: Massive programs and mandates will promise more than they can deliver. Selected people and programs that build on what is known and carefully share, assess, and adjust their knowledge and practice offer the best chance for success in a reasonable length of time.

National and state education leadership should work collaboratively to share understanding, knowledge of process, and outcome experiences. As in the Danish example, our state and national educational institutions need to provide incentives and sanctions in such a way that "we do not hurt the children."

Education affects every aspect of American life—our economic competitiveness, family functioning, child wellbeing, schooling, protection from outside attack, domestic tranquility, participation in civic life, and maintenance of our democracy. And good education requires good development. It is late in the day. We must promote education reform that puts child development front and center, quickly, or face a downhill future.

Work, Family, and Community

A number of people have asked me how and why I stuck to the same effort for 40 years, and I am surprised by their surprise. I have considered it a rare privilege to be able to use my entire career to address issues that are at the core of my being. It seems so logical and right to me that all young people should have the same opportunity in life that I had. It is what the American Dream is all about. Thus, my work has meaning and provides a sense of purpose to me, and now urgency, that goes far beyond academic or financial rewards. Given the opportunity to contribute a little bit toward helping the young and the country, why should I not keep plugging away?

Yes, the resistance and inertia is frustrating, particularly because the evidence keeps mounting that investments in supporting good development of the young cost far less than not doing so and would greatly improve our quality of life and the ability of our society to remain one of the most successful societies in the history of the world. And I am tenacious by nature. Also, much of my motivation is rooted in a very deep place.

I have often thought about the time that one of the three friends I began kindergarten with came by to wish me well when I was about to go off to college. As he was leaving, he continued to talk through a screen door that separated me in our kitchen from him on our back porch. I observed a tear trickle down from his eye. I was too choked up to speak. But this was more than two friends parting. I had a sensation of us standing on the caboose of two trains headed in different directions—one toward opportunity, and the other not. It was not until my internship 8 years later that I fully realized what was going on that day. It was the realization that many such outcomes were not necessary that first fueled my determination to promote opportunity, and continues to fuel it despite great resistance and inertia.

While the integration of child and adolescent development principles into all aspects of education has not happened often enough, many of the outcomes have been extraordinarily rewarding: the mother who was energized by SDP and returned to finish high school, went on to obtain a master's degree, and provided family support that enabled one daughter to become a doctor, another a lawyer, and two sons to become engineers; the parent who gained confidence and skills and went from public welfare to becoming a telephone operator supervisor; the school principal who told me that she had been a student in one of our pilot schools; a principal who insists that SDP saved his life because he had had a heart attack unsuccessfully trying to control his school and later did so with less stress as a facilitating leader; the prominent education leader who told his audience that my work first helped him realize that the motivation for academic learning was largely relational; and many more expressions of appreciation from students, parents, teachers, administrators, and policymakers. I am hugely gratified by these outcomes and responses. They far outweigh the frustration.

Also, the work has never been boring, and if I am not looking at the headlights of an oncoming train, I think I see light at the end of the tunnel. The voice for a focus on more than test scores—the whole child—is growing more persistent and louder every day.

Our SDP is usually classified as a comprehensive school reform model. And it is. But to me, after we were able to fashion the model from an authentic school improvement effort through the transfer of child and adolescent knowledge and skills, I have thought of our work as a probe.

We used our intervention efforts to answer the question of why schools were not successful with my able friends and others like them, and how to help bring about changes that will enable most to be successful in school and in life. These efforts led to interactions with and a better understanding of the many components of the education enterprise— schools of education, state departments of education, school boards, unions, foundations, political and other policymakers at the local, state and national levels.

I have thought of failure as a temporary option, as well as a step along the way to success. We've learned from every less-than-desired outcome and have worked with others in the education enterprise to move around obstacles and toward more effective interventions. And the most challenging task of all was to survive over 40 years while promoting adequate attention to child and adolescent development in an environment in which almost everybody—teachers, parents, administrators, funders, practice leaders, and policymakers—focused almost exclusively on curriculum, instruction, and assessment.

And finally, there was family. Was there a high cost of my effort that sometimes bordered on obsession? Fortunately, family was a part of the solution. I've already discussed the role of my family of origin. My family of procreation was equally important. My wife of 35 years, Shirley, passed away in 1994. But it was her strong support of me, our two children, our family life, and my career that made the early and very difficult years possible. About 20 years ago, against my better mind, substituting for a colleague, I gave a painfully bad speech in Germany on a topic I did not know enough about. I was rescued by a participant who asked me to say something about SDP, which then became the discussion centerpiece. Later, with a wry smile, Shirley said, "Whew, you were saved by the bell! But that was a great recovery!" Always, my pain, joy, and achievement were hers, and vice-versa. And as my daughter said in remembrance, "She was the glue that held our family together."

But I did my part. When our children were very young, I encountered adolescents who were probably paying the price for the fame and fortune their parents had achieved. I was determined to be there for our children as much as possible, despite my constant over-commitment. I put my son Brian's football and track schedule and my daughter Dawn's theater schedule—and all their activities—on my calendar first and scheduled my work around their dates. Until they were off to college I would not accept any out-of-town engagements on the weekends.

We had family-and-friend tailgate parties at every Yale home game during all their growing up years. On several occasions, I attended Brian's football game on Saturday morning, Yale's game in the afternoon, and then my son and I would go to the New York Giants games on Sunday during the year they played in the Yale Bowl. I like sports. In fact, I played in pick-up games at the Yale gym when I was a psychiatric resident, until I couldn't keep up with the speed and stamina of those young kids. I'm still on the Yale Faculty Athletic Committee. I enjoy the way team sports mimic life.

In short, my advice to the young researcher or academic is: Follow your question as best you can, even when different and demanding ways are required, but manage your life and family relationships and activities so that they serve as a rich source of motivation and strength during the good times and the bad. I'm told that I did not get the family thing perfect, but for a man of my generation, I wasn't bad. When my daughter, at about 13 years old, proclaimed me sexist, I reminded her of my earlier insistence that she have the same opportunities as her brother. She listened and re-membered, but said, "Well, you were ahead of your time then, but behind the times now!" I am now the cheerleader for her two feisty daughters and my son's son, who are busy giving their parents "the business" the way my children gave it to me.

I enjoy family and friends, and I continue to enjoy my work—that is the secret to my "success."

Circa 1962.
At UCLA.

Circa 1990.
At Skyline Marina in Anacortes, WA.

Circa 1986.
John and Lynn Goodlad.

John I. Goodlad

·ᴗ

Developing an Educative Ecology of Mind

John Goodlad spent his early years in the hills of North Vancouver, Canada, and graduated from North Vancouver High School with majors in fastpitch softball and soccer. After earning his teaching license from Vancouver Provincial Normal School, he went on to teach in a one-room school, served as teacher and principal of a small school, and spent 4 years as teacher and director of education in the Provincial Industrial School for Boys (a "reform" school). During these years, he earned his B.A. and M.A. at the University of British Columbia. Thus armed, John, along with his wife, Lynn, set out for a Ph.D. program at the University of Chicago. The next 38 years took him from Emory University and Agnes Scott College in Atlanta, back to a professorship at the University of Chicago, and then on to UCLA as a professor, director of the laboratory school, and, for 16 years, dean of the Graduate School of Education.

In 1983, John and Lynn attempted to retire on one of the San Juan Islands, just across the border from where they grew up in Canada. Retirement was to last only a few months, however, and most of that time was spent dealing with the media attention from the publication of *A Place Called School*. Unexpectedly, an interesting offer came from the University of Washington, and Lynn and John found themselves spending the so-called Golden Years in Seattle and the San Juans, where they could occasionally see the sun's rays striking the hills of North Vancouver. At the University of Washington, John and colleagues created the Center for Educational Renewal, the National Network for Educational Renewal, the Agenda for Education in a Democracy, and the nonprofit Institute for Educational Inquiry.

٠ﮯ

Just before his death, one of my mentors, educator Ralph Tyler, told an interviewer: "At bedtime each day, I ask myself three questions: What did I learn today, what does it mean, and how shall I use it?"

Clearly, he was thinking about using what he had learned that day to educate others. He was adding to his *educational* ecology that which might enrich the intentionally *educative* component of his mind. He was storing away information and ideas he perceived to be useful for his own varied teaching of others. And so, my purpose here is to put before you some knowledge I have found over the years to be useful in my efforts to enhance the learning of others. For readers who may wish to follow these fingerposts further, I provide references to some of my writings that accompanied experiences along the trail, the most comprehensive of which is *Romances with Schools: A Life of Education.*[1]

Woodward Hill School

Nearly everything I've learned about educating the young in schools was cultivated in a one-room rural school.

I came to what I was now beginning to learn with 19 years and 15 days of life and learning behind me. Nature and culture had already shaped many of my beliefs.[2] Walking in the unseasonably cold September morning drizzle toward Woodward Hill School in Surrey Municipality of southwestern British Columbia, I became aware that many of my new family of 34 pupils were already huddled on the front stoop.

I unlocked the door and, to their surprise, invited them in out of the cold and wet. Soon, the familiar odor of hot wool clothing was rising from those who had quickly positioned themselves near the pot-bellied stove that Mr. McKay, our janitor, had stoked and lit earlier. With no directives from me, most of the class had settled into their desks, the 1st-grade children in the row paralleling the windows, the 8th-grade youths along the inner chalkboard wall, and the rest in rows between. The array was almost entirely as I had charted our little room in my planning. I had wasted my time preparing it.

All my pupils save 4 of the 5 first graders had been here before. It was much more their school than mine. My recognition of this fact proved to be useful, not just for my stay in this school but for all my career to come. Students know best about what is good and bad in their schools, yet their views are rarely sought. Building on this early educative learning, I eventually concluded that one of the most productive ways to renew our schools is to get rid of many systemics and regularities that hardened into place decades ago in order to create space for the many good ideas and practices that have been unable to find entry.

For the first 6 weeks with my new "family," ages 6 to almost 18, I prepared, if one might call it that, 50 or more "lessons" each day. While visiting the school several weeks before, I had discovered that there were only a few old textbooks and a mouse nest in the book cupboard. Nothing had changed when I arrived in September, except that the mice and their nest were gone. What to do?

All I had to guide my teaching were three quite thick syllabi detailing the prescribed curricula. There were, however, chalkboards across the front, side, and back walls along with a box of chalk. And so, when the pupils had gone home on that first day, I wrote from left to right for hours before and after dinner (in the farmhouse where I boarded), leaving an open rectangular space at the front of the class for spelling lessons. Given eight grades and six or seven subjects per grade, my writing for each day usually ended at about 10 o'clock and covered all available chalkboard space. I found it necessary to continue this procedure even after getting my small allotment of books.

Soon, I discovered that during most discussions with the 8 eighth graders, the twins in the seventh grade had also joined us. Then, pupils in lower grades were unable to restrain their responses to questions I raised with the older students, and often the younger pupils' responses were as good as or better than the older ones'. What should I do? Then, there was the problem of teaching four of my 6-year-olds to read, something for which my student teaching had taught me little. One first grader, Ernie, was beginning his eighth year in the same seat in the same row. He had not learned to read, and most of his age-mates were now in the eighth grade. No previous teacher had known what to do and neither did I, except to hasten to get him a desk geared to his size. He liked the desk, but his lack of learning and his frequent soft moaning haunted me. What to do?

I had learned in normal school to follow a daily, graded curriculum that was designed to implement the syllabi, and I did not have the courage to break from this mode of planning. However, when I was getting into my second month at my one-room school house, I was tired and bored with it. Philosopher, friend, and former colleague Gary Fenstermacher once asked: "What would teaching and learning look like if it accorded with the highest ideals of which the human species is capable?"[3] Nowhere in my academic preparation to become an educator did I confront precisely this question, but something close to it surged forth in primitive formulation 6 weeks into my stewardship of Woodward Hill School.

Each Friday in the late afternoon, I journeyed by interurban train to spend the weekend with my mother in Vancouver. At this time, my only social life was during the usual soccer game played each Saturday afternoon. One Saturday evening, I was struck by a kind of soaring epiphany. As I kicked the kitchen door, my mind landed back in my classroom.

In the eighth grade, we were about to enter into a unit of study about our province, British Columbia. Most of my first graders were struggling to learn to read the Dick and Jane stuff in their textbook readers. The middle grade students were laboring to learn to add, subtract, multiply, and divide in sequence rather than together (something that struck me as rather odd later on). The several boys and girls in the fifth grade were about to enjoy a wonderful text on the Chinook salmon. Wasn't all this clutter connected in some way?

Of course! I needed an integrative organizing center! What might it be? I envisioned my classroom again. The desks were fastened to skids, three to a cluster and easily moved about; the aisles between them could be narrowed. I could create an 8- to 10-foot space along the inside wall opposite the windows where I could fit a long table with boards fencing in the top. Then, I could line it with waterproof material and fill it halfway with sand, and we would have our curricular organizing center. When Mr. McKay finished building the center the following weekend, everyone in my classroom family was intrigued. During the first few days, mixed-age groups learned about the geography and topography of British Columbia on the sand table. Later, the mighty Fraser River found its way through the sand table's mountains to its lush delta. The tributaries where salmon would spawn each fall flowed into the river. Then, logging towns came into being. Ernie proved himself to be a careful topographer, working with his upper-grade peers for the first time in years. Bright but delicate Esther took advantage of sand table opportunities to be side by side with her heroine, Helen, our 13-going-on-18-year-old motherly sage.

The barrenness of our one cupboard did not matter. Books, pictures, a wide array of construction materials, canned salmon, and various pieces of bric-a-brac were supplied from the students' homes. I already had Helen and Oliver helping me with the reading instruction, and now the process similar to the teaching of younger brothers and sisters by older siblings came into full play. We were a learning community.

Fortunately, I held on to my daily teaching of spelling and arithmetic, the two subjects of the syllabi that appeared to be the most graded. I was not accountable to a principal because I was the principal, and there was no district superintendent or staff. But a provincial school inspector would be around in due time. His black Ford coupe came quietly alongside our front stairs 2 weeks after I had broken away from many of the regularities of schooling. I knew that a negative report to the school board might finish my teaching career in Surrey Municipality. When he arrived, I was surprised to be greeting the same gentle, stooped, gray-of-face-and-dress inspector who had visited North Star School, the first school I had ever attended and where I had barely escaped flunking the first grade.

The inspector, Mr. Calvert, was intrigued with our sand table. He asked if I was familiar with "progressive" educators such as John Dewey and William Heard Kilpatrick. Walking to his car later, he smiled his slow, enigmatic smile, which one could interpret many different ways. "Mr. Goodlad," he said, "I very much like what you are doing. Just always make sure that your pupils do well in arithmetic."

Transition

Leaving Woodward Hill School was not an easy parting. Nonetheless, I accepted an unexpected offer of a "promotion" to White Rock Elementary School, still in the Surrey Municipal School District. Two big attractions were that I could live in a front room in the little White Rock Lodge facing the beach of Semiahmoo Bay and that my room and board would cost less than my present circumstances. My *annual* salary of $780 would rise to $800, out of which I would be endeavoring to save $200 for summer school.

The next couple of years took me from thinking of schooling solely in terms of classroom teaching to thinking of schooling as a political, economic, sociological, cultural enterprise. Without realizing it, I guess that I took a small step toward developing a little skill in the sort of "crap-detecting" that Neil Postman and Charles Weingartner recommended that all educators should acquire.[4]

Halfway through my first year there, a new junior high school (an innovation at the time) opened next to the elementary school. It was short of the space needed. Given that the higher grades almost always take precedence over the lower, my classroom was taken over. I had the good fortune to be shunted to a one-room church building a couple of miles away. I say "good fortune" because I was back to a one-room school, this time with only the fourth and fifth grades, and once again I had almost full agency over my teaching. The elementary school principal was new and comfortably relaxed in his management. He was a teaching principal and did not find time to visit me. Mr. Calvert did not come by during the several months the children and I were there creating our own learning community.

The following year, I became the teaching principal of a new elementary school in the fast-growing northwest corner of Surrey, just across the Fraser River from New Westminster. There was no community as of yet, just new houses in various stages of construction. There were no stores, gas stations, and motels; no place for me to board; and no automobiles to take me to the school or anywhere else. My annual salary became $1,020, the approximate cost of a small car. My 1 year there capped a 3-year apprenticeship of teaching in public schools.

In retrospect, it is easy to understand why the second and third of these 3 years generated no budding hypotheses I could come to believe in. The Woodward Hill experience provided the incentive—the near necessity—for my later research on grade promotion and nonpromotion, which eventually led to my belief in nongrading. As James B. Conant, nominee for a Nobel Prize because of his research on photosynthesis, wrote in a little book entitled *My Credo,* a scientist would not spend a career on the trail of a hypothesis unless she or he believed in its ultimate confirmation. A couple of hypotheses did begin to bounce around in my mind during 4 subsequent years of teaching in a very different kind of school—an institution intended to "reform" the behavior of delinquent boys under the age of 18.

What did emerge again and again during this 7-year apprenticeship in elementary and secondary school-keeping were questions about the schooling enterprise; in effect, the larger gestalt of schools and their cultural context. Together, the genesis of a few hypotheses and a clutch of questions about the schooling enterprise shaped for me more than 6 subsequent decades of inquiry, satisfaction, and gratitude for the roads not taken.

I enjoyed enormous freedom throughout my apprenticeship years. Had the No Child Left Behind Act of today been in effect when I was at Woodward Hill School, would I have risked the sand table? I think not. Would I have quit teaching at the end of that year? I think so. Would I have profited from a teacher mentor visiting me for a few hours each week? I think not. Should the syllabi have been much more specific, perhaps specifying the daily curriculum? No. Would I have profited more from being a physical presence each day at White Rock Elementary instead of a lone teacher in my church school? Probably not. I view my freedom throughout my first 7 years as being heaven sent. Would school administrators and policymakers agree or disagree? Would I have profited from a more comprehensive teacher education program, grounded in foundations focused on developing my educative ecology of mind and interspersed with practice? Yes, indeed. Such questions will continue to surface whenever the reform or renewal of teacher education is in fashion.

A question arose out of my misconception of the necessary role of a school principal. I thought a principal was supposed to provide leadership regarding the overall functioning of the school. After a couple of weeks spent establishing the rhythm of my class, I turned my attention to some matters pertaining to school safety, the scheduling of recess and use of the playground, the comfort and possible discomfort of the teachers with the grading practices that were in place, and more. As a principal, what should I be doing about these issues, if anything?

I called a meeting after the usual clearing out of our pupils. The teachers—all female—settled uncomfortably and mute into the upper-grade desks, clasping their purses and wearing their coats. Apparently, they were anticipating a short meeting on administrative matters. The senior teacher, whom I later observed to be first-rate and better prepared to be a principal than I, continued to show the same sort of animosity toward me she evidenced by never saying more than "good morning" to me when we met in the hallway. I knew that I had been chosen initially for the Woodward Hill position because I was male and had a modest background in sports. This meeting—our first and last—ended in a half hour because everything that came up apparently was my responsibility and they resented the prospect of "helping me." This experience still troubles me.

Another troubling question is more encompassing: What are schools for, anyway, and how should they go about advancing their proper mission, unavoidably a moral one? This question and several more of vital importance always will be awaiting educators, offering them an interesting, satisfying life of education in pursuit of an answer. However, early in the journey of exploration, it will become apparent that such encompassing questions never will be answered at a high level of satisfaction by educators alone and that these questions are closely tied to the care of our democracy. The agenda to be developed is nonnegotiable and can be forwarded successfully only if they are advanced by policymakers, educators, and local communities working together. I think I began to be at least a little aware of the significance, the necessity, of this agenda during the concluding 4 years of my apprenticeship in teaching the young.

BISCOQ

Nearly everything else I've learned about educating the young was cultivated in a boys' reform school.

I spent much more time as director of education in the British Columbia Industrial School for (delinquent) Boys in Port Coquitlam (BISCOQ) than I did in Woodward Hill School. My brief stint as a teaching principal taught me a lot about why the deep structure of schooling, with its accompanying symbols, is so difficult to change. At BISCOQ, I was acutely aware of how institutional culture shaped my agency not only as a teacher but also as a human being.

The school was without fences and located close to the main road. Quick-footed boys, in the brief interlude between, for example, a morning class with me or a session on tailoring with Mr. Henderson, occasionally sprinted to the road and raised a thumb to get a lift from a passing car. If they were not successful, they returned for the lunchtime roll call.

At that time, the no-security Borstal system for late teen and young adult offenders in England was being considered in British Columbia as a way station between the industrial school (earlier termed "reform school") and the penitentiary. This signaled the possibility of a shift in ideology at BISCOQ from "once a bad boy, always a bad boy" to "these boys need support, care, and education" to turn them into good adult citizens. It also split the staff into two camps, each with a strong leader. Hugh Christie, the relatively new deputy superintendent who was immersed in social work and criminology studies at the University of British Columbia, was a superb representative of the more progressive position. Syd Evans, third in command, firm and competent and commonly regarded as fair, had for years advanced the dominant belief in the intractability of the bad-from-birth syndrome. Straddling the abyss was Superintendent George Ross, an amiable man who abhorred conflict and whose management style was sharply influenced by news of the school reaching the press and politicians. He must have been troubled quite a bit on those occasions when Mrs. Ross, driving to town, would pick up a couple of hitchhiking runaways who had failed to recognize her and cheerfully chat with them while returning them to BISCOQ. A report of this in the local newspaper would be devastating.

What I learned from my 4 years at BISCOQ about the culture of schooling and the problem of change—to borrow from the title of Seymour Sarason's engaging book[5]—would fill many more chapters than this one. The richness of what I stored away in my ecology of educative belief came in part from the rawness of institutional culture and the social and political surroundings. How does one develop and sustain personal and professional agency geared toward the moral underpinnings of our democracy when he or she is surrounded by cultural deterrents? How should I respond to opposing views without setting back the progress

Christie was making in renewing the culture of BISCOQ? Is it best in such situations to challenge opposing views, remain silent, and ignore the frequent question, "How are the bad boys on the funny farm?" Friend and colleague philosopher Lyle Eddy introduced the core issue to his university classes in very simple language: "When your wife comes home with a new hat you strongly dislike, do you tell her the truth or that you like it very much?"

With friends and others outside of the BISCOQ culture, I challenged their opposing positions on juvenile delinquency. But inside this culture, where the stakes were high, the divisions in belief were clear and required little vocal defense. We tried to practice our beliefs in our daily work, avoiding conflict to the degree possible.

One of the things I was trying to accomplish in my teaching was the development of what today would be called a learning community. My class was steadily increasing in size because boys over the compulsory school attendance age of 16 were now joining us. I was further stretched into the secondary school curriculum to the point where another teacher was justified. My new half-time colleague and I split the morning shift into upper- and lower-elementary school classes. I then taught the secondary-level students in the afternoon, aided magnificently by the province's extension program.

Since I had secured my Bachelor of Arts degree entirely through summer school and the extension program of the University of British Columbia and was now following the same route in advancing toward the master's degree, the students and I had much in common. We constituted a community of goal-centered individuals. The deep structure of graded schooling was abandoned.

We had a good year, my third at BISCOQ. Nearing its end, we talked about some kind of celebration that would involve our entire classroom community. The boys wanted an off-campus picnic that would begin late in the afternoon and allow us to get back in time for the pre-bedtime check. I would need permission, and the political stakes demanded caution. Christie had the necessary authority, but he would be blamed for anything that went wrong. How might I ensure that I alone would bear the blame? I knew I had to jump over both Hugh and Syd Evans who also had approval authority.

Early on at BISCOQ, I was beginning to learn a little about the difference between regarding superiors as political facilitators and as authoritarians. And so I visited with George Ross every month or two in order to tell him how things were going. He appeared to enjoy these conversations, perhaps because I never brought him problems to solve or requested permission for changes I was making in the classrooms. Faced with the matter of the proposed picnic scheduled to take place in a couple of weeks, I had a conversation with Mr. Ross about the good year my colleague and I were having, thanked him again for his role in easing my work load by adding my half-time colleague, and told him about the picnic we were planning. I did not ask permission and he neither approved nor disapproved. The picnic was a great success, but Syd Evans let it be known that he strongly disapproved nonetheless.

We planned another the following year. This time permission was not an issue. We had made a small dent in the culture of BISCOQ; nothing like it had occurred before. Again, Syd Evans expressed his discontent, and because several recent runaways had attracted public attention, Christie added an additional chaperone.

Things might have gone better if my fellow teacher and I had been the only chaperones. BISCOQ was not a place of serious cross-cultural discourse. The three of us on the staff took advantage of the opportunity to talk, staying together with our eyes taking in the open field and the ongoing activities, or so we thought. Two of the boys slipped away unseen to a house unknown to us hidden in the adjacent woods, found an unlocked window, and took some money. I learned of the escapade at breakfast the following morning. The culprits had already been identified and were confined in the school's security room. Evans, who had been on night duty, kept the news to himself until most of the dining room chairs were filled and then reminded us that he had told us so.

The blame was all mine. Nobody of higher authority was reprimanded. I do not know how George Ross handled the press and public. I was told not to do it again. Interestingly, Evans's repeated "I told you so" got rather subdued attention. In the weeks that followed, colleagues on both sides of our ideological schism came out of the woodwork to give me quiet commendation. Perhaps my interpretation was wrong, but they seemed to be saying that the good health of our institution required greater freedom of both individual and group agency so that the boundaries of our beliefs and actions might receive greater attention and perhaps expand.

BISCOQ was an intense, ordered environment with clearly established cultural norms. My break with these norms might appear to the reader to have been modest, but to those of us on the inside, it was much more. The first picnic aroused a kind of curious apprehension on both sides of the ideological divide, punctuated by the warnings of Syd Evans. The second picnic strengthened the established norms but aroused on both sides sudden awareness of the restrictive social and political environment these norms created. I think that the surprising sympathetic support I received grew out of awareness that some of the cultural norms could and should be changed. Indeed, we might rise above the bantering debate and take action on some of the ideas Hugh Christie put forward.

For the first 3 years of my life at BISCOQ, I lived there from Sunday evening to late Friday afternoon each week in a tiny suite next to the two classrooms. Two weeks before the beginning of the fourth year, I got married. I then commuted to and from Vancouver each weekday. My waking hours were no longer encased in the routines of BISCOQ. I could back off, get a clearer perspective, and reflect.

Up to that year, my educative thoughts were tied to the daily work schedule. Tyler's three questions—What did I learn today, what does it mean, and how shall I use it?—would have filled my educative ecology of mind if I had known of them then. At the start, I had viewed the boys as my pupils. Now I began to see them as members of humankind: all of one people in the total that is humanity. How challenged I would have been with the question raised more than 6 decades later by Gary Fenstermacher: "What would teaching and learning look like if it accorded with the highest ideals of which the human species is capable?" How does one go about answering such a question?

Juvenile delinquents constitute one more group for which there appears to be no place in the human ecosystem. The answer to this problem is clear, of course: from before birth, every child must have caring parents, a comfortable home, and the support of a social and political democracy. Are these bounties not a large part of the American dream? We will not have these conditions by concentrating solely on the well-being of individuals. If our culture is to ensure the education each of us must have for satisfying, responsible, healthful self-realization, we must accept that our schools are tools for intentionally developing the democratic public of an educative culture.

Most of the boys at BISCOQ were brought back a second or third time over a period of 2 or 3 years. Some who were there when I came waved me goodbye on my leaving 4 years later. During their absences, they were rarely part of an educative culture. Indeed, often they were automatically suspects when an automobile was stolen or a home broken into in their neighborhoods. Hugh Christie and I agreed that the culture of our school was not sufficiently powerful to end recidivism. At best, it was a protective sanctuary that had no positive impact on the norms of the larger surround. More and more, Hugh turned his attention to figuring out what had to change outside of BISCOQ if norms of recidivism were to be no more.

I have not seen or talked with Hugh Christie since I left, but I have heard that his enlightened vision gained more and more support in the infrastructure of the province. If I were to meet Syd Evans again, I would try to hold back from saying, "I told you so."

Beyond Apprenticeship

Nearly everything else educative that clutters my mind today either is derivative of those early years or crept into my thinking from my adventures in institutions of higher learning and education in the culture beyond. The sources are varied and many.

Three months after leaving BISCOQ, my wife, Lynn, and I were crossing the Rocky Mountains on our way to Chicago and one of the world's great universities: she with a permanent resident visa, thanks to one of life's little bureaucratic miracles, and I with a 2-year student visa. We presumed that, after the passage of these 2 years, we would be back in British Columbia, where I would complete the dissertation requirement for a Ph.D. at the University of Chicago. Things change.

A week into my studies, I was so deep in reading in the departmental library of Judd Hall that I sometimes forgot to attend scheduled classes. What an intellectual and emotional treat! But the pressures were great. That 2-year time limit loomed over my head so greatly that I elected to

take the several most critical exams for entry into the Ph.D. program after completing only three of the nine courses that were believed to be the
best preparation for those exams.

My time in the lap of academe was even shorter than anticipated.
On a hot summer's day, four academic quarters later, my faculty advisor, Virgil Herrick, suggested that I talk with a visitor. The visitor,
Floyd Jordan, director of the Atlanta Area Teacher Education Service
(AATES), was recruiting experienced educators studying for advanced
degrees. The educators who were chosen would be awarded fellow-
ships funded by the Ford Foundation and would work half time in the
program, leaving the other half of their time for their dissertations. A
couple of months later, Lynn and I were on our way to Atlanta, and so
closed an awesome year for a couple of kids from western Canada. We
thought we were going to Atlanta for 1 year; we stayed for 8½.

The AATES was a product of *local need,* a need rapidly rising throughout the nation. Local need is, I think, the necessary driving force behind
innovation and change, whether in schools or in other components of
community infrastructure. It was a superb example of renewing the teaching force through university and school district collaboration, a should-be-
obvious concept for major improvement of teacher education.

In the immediate aftermath of World War II, a startlingly large
proportion of the U.S. teaching force did not hold university degrees.
Lawrence Haskew, head of the division of teacher education at Emory
University, came up with the idea of partnering half a dozen institutions
of higher education with their surrounding school districts in order to
provide readily accessible degree programs for the districts' teachers. The
AATES coordinated the whole, engaging faculty members at the several
institutions to teach the necessary courses (as part of their regular loads)
in district schools to teachers who earned credits with their chosen universities. (Teacher Y of Cobb County school district, for example, might
take a class in downtown Atlanta taught by a professor of Emory University and credit it to her degree program at the University of Georgia
in Athens.) Each year, Floyd Jordan consulted with school district officials, who in turn polled teachers for recommendations for the next year's
courses. Several of the participating universities' departments took the
lead in revising their regular programs with future and in-service teach-

ers in mind. The Department of Art at the University of Georgia, for example, launched a renaissance in the arts and arts education that spread to schools throughout the state.

The venture was successful because it met this public need, which had considerable social, economic, and community significance. Yet there were other states with a similar need. What did they do? My guess is that they did the usual, hired temporary, probably inadequately prepared teachers of teachers to take care of enrollment overload. Why did the concept of collaboration of departments in the arts and sciences, colleges of education, and cooperating partner schools not come forward into the improvement of teacher education for another half century? Why did the AATES settle into its founding mode and never become a renewing institution? Questions of this sort increasingly clouded my mind.

My fellow colleagues and I seemed to become aware at about the same time that other possibilities for the AATES should be explored. The carrying of university classes out to schools in the late afternoon was often cited as an instructional innovation. But the only benefit was improved accessibility of the courses. Jordan liked our ideas but saw them as beyond the scope of the AATES.

The AATES had been for several years host to one of the nationwide settings of the Daniel Prescott Child Study Program, an interesting initiative that appears not to have found its way into the history of American schooling. Prescott had put together a 3-year sequence for experienced teachers that began with each teacher studying a single young pupil for an entire academic year. Headquartered at the University of Maryland, the program wisely brought together the setting leaders who joined Prescott in intensive seminars. The leader in the Atlanta area, Lynn Shufelt—commonly addressed as Pat—was a colleague in the AATES.

A few years after coming to Atlanta, when I was increasingly absorbed with my professorial and administrative responsibilities at Agnes Scott College and Emory University, Pat invited me to join him in creating a fourth year of the Prescott initiative, a year that would be devoted to graduates of the first 3 years and draw out implications for practice from what they had learned. It was an interesting proposal that these experienced teachers, Pat, and I approached with enthusiasm. But the year was one of frustration for all and was, Pat and I agreed, a failure.

Initial frustration grew out of the teachers' perception that little of what they might want to change in their classrooms could be accomplished without changes in their schools' circumstances. More serious was their growing realization that they were having great difficulty reaching back into their studies of childhood and accompanying seminars to draw out implications for curricula and instruction. They had done some of this in their seminars but had not pushed far because, apparently, they had considered the exercise to be somewhat of a digression.

Why had they not, during those earlier years, been tucking hypotheses into their respective ecologies of educative belief? Must the development of understanding be linear? My thoughts turned to the linear nature of most professional educational programs. During their child study program, had these teachers not asked themselves Ralph Tyler's simple question from time to time: How shall I use what I learned today? Is integration of practice and relevant concept and principle not possible?

Renewal and the Culture of Schooling

The more I got into the culture of higher education, the more I missed that of the lower schools. I longed to test some of the hypotheses that had been taking shape in my mind, not through inquiry alone but through implementation laced with inquiry—which I saw more and more to be the stuff of school renewal. For this I would need some agency with a school, much as I had during my apprenticeship years.

For me, the superiority of nongraded over graded schools was no longer a hypothesis; it was a belief. I guess it was my haunting memory of Ernie that determined my selection of a doctoral dissertation that confirmed my earlier observations regarding the misfit between individual differences among humans and the graded school. My data from studying two matched groups of children, one retained in the first grade for a year and the other promoted to the second, favored the latter significantly, but their respective experiences of the year served neither well. My conclusion and recommendation was to get rid of both promotion and nonpromotion through the creation of nongraded schools.[6] How might we do that?

The opportunity came unexpectedly, as had my other career opportunities up to that point. My friend Bob Anderson called. He had conducted a study, funded by Mr. and Mrs. William Vanderbilt, of the Englewood School in Sarasota County, Florida. The Vanderbilts had fallen in love with nearby Manasota Key but not the school that their son attended during their long stays on the key. The school district superintendent and they agreed on the implementation of Bob's recommendations resulting from a project he had directed. But he was now a professor at Harvard and a considerable distance from Englewood. I was much closer in Atlanta. He asked if I would take over. Yes, I thought, I would. I particularly liked the idea of becoming a hybrid educator, engaged responsibly in the cultures of both higher education and public schooling.

Several years into the Englewood Project, I accepted a professorship at the University of Chicago. Lynn, our two children, and I spent the spring quarter of each of 4 subsequent years in Englewood, a wonderful release from Chicago's winter climate. The impact of those Chicago winters on our son Stephen's health, and to some degree on mine, entered into another gut-wrenching decision: I accepted an unexpected offer to go to the University of California at Los Angeles (UCLA). My professorship there embraced the directorship of the university's prestigious elementary laboratory school, the University Elementary School (UES). It was time to break the long relationship with the Englewood School, but I would continue my hybrid educator experiences in a new setting.

Chapter nine of *Romances with Schools* is devoted to my perception of what transpired over several years of intentional renewal of two very different schools in two very different subcultures of the United States. Several colleagues at the University of Chicago had put forward the proposition that it would be very difficult, if not impossible, to nongrade a largely upper-middle-class school, particularly given the parents' expectations that their children would attend prestigious colleges. They were wrong. There were pitfalls to be avoided at the UES that did not exist at Englewood—for example, the UES parents expected more information about everything we were doing—but the entire process of renewal moved along more smoothly than I had expected.

Our move to California took place 3 years after Sputnik I and II had circled the globe and ushered in what I refer to in *Romances with Schools* as "the schooling decade." The well-received 1959 Conant report on high schools did not shatter the nation's faith, but along with the scientific advancement of the U.S.S.R., it did generate unprecedented political interest in school reform, which ultimately weakened support for our internationally admired experiment in universal public schooling.

I hated the concept of school *reform* from the time of its emergence and have urged educators to disown it except when referring to its use by others. No doubt my antipathy goes back to the BISCOQ years. School reform is a nasty concept; "reform" is defined by my Webster's dictionary as "amendment of what is defective, vicious, corrupt, or depraved." What an insult to throw at stewards of schooling! My conception of school *renewal,* which aims at improving our educational institutions, is vastly different.

School reform will never give us the schools our democracy must have. *Reform* is a companion of the mechanistic, Industrial-Age, command-and-control model of organizational behavior that has been challenged again and again by thoughtful analysts for its dehumanization of the workplace and, indeed, work itself. *Renewal* is a radical departure from that model, fitting more with systems, complexity, and perhaps chaos theories, which have been discouragingly slow to enter the schooling enterprise. Business leader Dee Hock has coined the word *chaordic* in describing the emerging age of chaos, complexity, and necessary order in which "the second digital" decade Bill Gates talks about will be only a part, admittedly an important one.

A quotation from Hock's book, which describes his story of making possible what appeared time and again to be impossible, connects me with my experiences with sustained school renewal: "The truth is that, given the right chaordic circumstances, from no more than dreams, determination, and the liberty to try, quite ordinary people consistently do extraordinary things."[7] The common practice of trying to replicate some existing, perceived model, whether or not mandated, is doomed to fail—even if bits and pieces of it come into being. The major goal in renewal is to establish the right chaordic circumstances—primarily cultural.

At our first meeting of the UES staff, many of the teachers came with copies of Bob Anderson's and my book, *The Nongraded Elementary School,* published the preceding year.[8] Near the meeting's end, I asked why. A little laughter accompanied the confession that they had expected me to include in my anticipated plan that we would, of course, nongrade. "Will we?" someone now boldly asked. I said I didn't know; we would take a hard look together at our strengths, weaknesses, and what we might begin to do about them. We would talk about our mission, the principles that should guide our work and that fit our mission, and the principles that did not.

How helpful it would have been if, for our early conversations, Dee Hock's story and book had been available. At one point in the story, he and his intimate friend, Old Monkey Mind (so much more creatively named than my "ecology of educative belief"), are thinking about the necessary redesign of organizations and institutions. He writes, "Every institution is interdependent with every other institution and with their social and physical environment. . . . Understanding requires mastery of four ways of looking at things—as they *were,* as they *are,* as they *might become,* and as they *ought to be.*"⁹

Leaving aside for a moment the wholeness of chaordic circumstances, the social and physical circumstances of institutions significantly influence the subsequent course of renewal. All settings differ. Serendipity had presented me with two schools that could not have differed more.

The most obvious need at Englewood was the development of community pride in the school, a goal nobody in or out of the school viewed as attainable. We began the impossible by bringing the school community together to ask the county, at long last, to construct a drainage system that would prevent the formation of the "pond" that took over most of the ground surrounding the school each rainy season. Nearly everything necessary to keep pride growing afterward was generated by a 3-minute conversation with Lee Zimmerman, the new principal I had chosen to take over the first September after my arrival. (Her predecessor had been appointed to a district office.)

I was greeting Lee in her little office when a boy came in with the daily mail. "Why don't you pick up the mail?" I asked her. "Because people would like to talk with me and I with them. It would take up too much of my time," she answered. "But," I said, "over that time, you would converse with nearly everyone in Englewood." From then on, several times a week, she did pick up the mail, profoundly increasing community interest and participation in the school. Sometimes the little things in renewal have big effects.

Getting the flow of renewal going at the UES, on the other hand, was a greater challenge. The school was already loved by parents and was well known beyond the community. Visitors came regularly to observe the hands-on learning about trading ships crossing the pond on our creek, which served as the Pacific Ocean; the construction activities with hammer and saw; the pueblo; the legendary curriculum of transportation; the westward movement of the nation's pioneers; the United Nations; and more. The fear of changing, rather than polishing, what existed was palpable.

I soon discovered that the school had hardened into place, albeit a place far ahead, in my judgment, of most schools in my experience. Early on, I visited classes daily, often asking the teachers why they were doing what they were doing. They began to view me as stupid. Again and again, I got simplistic answers. For example, I was told that the construction activity developed manual dexterity. I did not hear anything about its being an alternative approach to problem solving, nor any commentary on teamwork. I got the impression that much of what brought visitors to the school lacked clear educational purpose. Clearly, this was something the teachers and I needed to talk about—a good entry point for addressing the general absence of serious educative dialogue.

Perhaps because of their shorter teaching day, the cluster of teachers in the early childhood unit, which consisted of nursery school and kindergarten, engaged regularly in spirited conversation about their work. My "why" questions about bantams, balance boards, and other uncommon learning materials caused rather obvious concern over why such a stupid director of the school had been thrust upon them. However, when I pushed further and asked questions about how the children were reacting to their educational milieu, they began to understand what I was driving at. Soon, we were inquiring together about how we might get evidence to answer such questions. We began to meet regularly; the conversation was on a high plane of theory and practice.

I asked the wonderful acting principal Margaret Mathews about this striking difference between these teachers and the others in classes above who shied away from educative discourse. Her response opened a little passageway toward the beginning of a (chaordic) renewing mode in the culture of the progressive school the beloved founder, Miss Corinne Seeds, had crafted. Was the Yellow Brick Road that loomed before me a mirage?

According to Margaret (who knew the school's history well), Corinne Seeds had believed that early childhood was a time for play. If I am interpreting Margaret correctly and if her views were a valid interpretation, Miss Seeds regarded the function of the early childhood unit as providing thoughtful child care and safe play. She had delegated administrative responsibility to the vice principal, who, I believe, had taught regularly in the unit and still did when necessary. She and the teachers had expectations for it to be richly educational as well.

The expectation of the senior 1st-grade teacher was that the children would come to her from kindergarten "prepared." The two kindergarten teachers had a broader view of what "prepared" meant. What these three teachers and many parents did not want any longer was the division of the lower grades into half-grades: 1A and 1B, 2A and 2B, and so on. Some children got the message twice a year that they had failed. We were on our way down the Yellow Brick Road; nobody protested our elimination of the tracking practice. In fact, nobody seemed to know why it was started and then continued.

More changes quickly followed. Promotion from kindergarten to the first grade always had been automatic. Early childhood education (ECE) was not schooling, remember, it was play time. The ECE teachers invited the 1st-grade teachers to join them in making *deliberate decisions* about the 1st-grade class that were thought best for each child. For which of these alternatives did each appear to be best suited? That 1st-grade teacher who insisted on preparedness could even choose the children who would come to her. As things turned out, she went along with group decisions, as did her colleagues.

The familiar one-grade-per-class part of the deep structure of schooling simply collapsed, although we did not drop the grade designation. The third grade simply became the third year in school. Then Jimmy Nations, a relatively new teacher, proposed what he had longed for elsewhere: a one-room-school classroom. We did not quite manage to provide him with children of every age in his class, but we came close. The desire of other teachers to team-teach several grades together redesigned that beautiful grade-by-grade interior of the school a bit—we replaced some nonstructural walls with sliding or folding partitions.

It took a while for most of the teachers to comprehend and implement their new individual and collective agency within their increasingly democratic school culture. We thought together about what the UES *ought to become*. Increasingly, there was no perceived need to tread cautiously. We reinvigorated some of what the school had once been and some of what it still was, and we walked down the Yellow Brick Road into the very essence of what we hoped Miss Seeds's school would grow to be. We joined with the central administration of UCLA, parents, and friends in giving the school her name while she was still alive to savor her pride and appreciation.

Some Things That Beg Renewal

Historians are reluctant to analyze the recent past. Some insist on the passage of at least 50 years before they will attempt an analysis; others, usually reluctantly, only 20. Some of the hypotheses I generated early on now constitute belief; others are still bouncing around in my Old Monkey Mind, hopefully awaiting confirmation. What I now address is mostly inquiry that confirmed or strengthened my belief.

In spring 1965, Congress passed President Lyndon B. Johnson's Elementary and Secondary Education Act (ESEA), a far cry from the No Child Left Behind version of the Act passed by Congress nearly 4 decades later. It provided the largest federal budget ever for educational research and development. Title III provided, for the second time in my career, the idea of joining schools and universities in improving our schools. This time, the initiative was to be taken by schools that would seek collaborative involvement of higher education.

A steady stream of visitors came to visit the UES that was replacing much of the school that once was. Their reactions were much like those of visitors to the school years before: a laboratory school could do what they observed; their school back home could not. Following the 1965 ESEA, visitors came by the busload. Two years later, the UES faculty and I decided to explore whether we would find something "out there" different from what nearly all of our visitors were saying.

A \$7,500 grant from the Ford Foundation enabled us to do much more than expected. In our initial round of exploration, we visited 158 classrooms in 67 schools of 26 school districts scattered across the United States. Then we visited 27 classrooms in or near 7 cities of 4 southwestern states. Finally, we observed 75 classrooms in 31 schools of California, the classrooms chosen at random in schools identified as having reputations for innovation. Our 10 reasonable expectations, all addressed to the sort of instruction, learning, purposes, materials, classroom climate, and more that one might expect in good schools proved to be unreasonable.[10]

Schools and classrooms varied widely on all fronts, as we had expected. What troubled us most was the near uniform absence of schoolwide commitment to common purpose. Teachers, parents, and others appeared not to be working together toward developing either a sense of direction or solutions to schoolwide problems concerning them. In other words, there were not infrastructures for renewal. What should we do next? And then serendipity struck again.

A timely invitation from the Kettering Foundation provided me with the opportunity to explore the following burning questions that had their genesis in earlier experiences: Why were our schools not able to put together the obviously necessary conditions for even trying to change and renew? Was the need not obvious to the people responsible for schools' well-being? Were principals unable to provide the necessary leadership? Were teachers inadequately prepared for the task or prepared not at all? Did they not renew themselves?

The visit of two officers of the Kettering Foundation was a prelude to the Foundation's creation of the Institute for Development of Educational Activities (IDEA). Its purpose was comprehensive, to improve the nation's schooling in as many ways as possible. Subsequently, I was invited to head one of three divisions, that of research. Simultaneously, UCLA Chancellor Franklin Murphy was asking me to take a job I did not want: dean of the Graduate School of Education. A tough negotiator who was both visionary and charismatic, he twisted my arm with promises of resources to the school I could not ignore. When I still resisted because I was interested in the Kettering invitation, he shamed me into taking on that, too, by summarizing some of the things he did besides lead UCLA.

My first interest with IDEA was in finding out what it would take to help a diverse array of schools achieve a renewing culture without anyone involved having the sort of agency I had enjoyed with both the Englewood Project and the UES. This time, however, I would have the necessary resources for inquiry. Also, I would have my hands and head full with the deanship, the continued directorship of the UES, and my new responsibilities with IDEA.

A little group was needed to work with and study over time a clutch of "ordinary" schools. I recruited from across the country several experienced school-based educators who qualified for doctoral studies at UCLA and, from the local area, a small team of potential researchers, most of whom were able to take time off from childrearing or who were spouses of primary wage-earners. A colleague, Virgil Howes, took major responsibility for working with 18 school superintendents in selecting from each of their districts an "average" school that then became part of our fledgling network, the League of Cooperating Schools, stretching from San Diego on the south to Santa Barbara on the north and the San Bernardino Mountains on the east. Each school was assigned a "friend" from the UCLA group; the friends would share their observations with the researchers.

It soon became apparent that these schools were very much like those from which the visitors to the UES came and like those that colleagues and I had visited in the conduct of our earlier study. None of the schools had an ongoing structure designed to forward a continuous process of what our IDEA team came to call DDAE: *dialogue* about school purposes, problems, and issues; *decisions* regarding courses of action; subsequent *action;* followed by *evaluation* of the entire process—the core of the renewing process.

The principals of the schools and I agreed to meet for a full day on the first Monday of each month. The topic we had decided to discuss at the next meeting determined who from our IDEA staff would be required to attend it; others were welcome to participate if they so desired. The principals often played the role of teachers in their own schools, learning the DDAE process in, for example, addressing the topic of teachers' role as moral stewards of their schools. Early on, we struggled with the idea of schools' having a public purpose such as developing citizens who are responsible for the care of our democracy. Our ongoing research revealed that the topic had never been discussed in any of the 18 schools.

We had a wonderful 6-year run. The toughest goal for the principals was to take charge of their leadership roles without taking command. Moving into "working" agreements through the process of dialogue proved to be the most difficult part of the DDAE process. Some principals had trouble moving ahead into action when decisions were not unanimous but learned the art of revisiting them if objections continued. There was eagerness to learn how to lead without controlling.

I became convinced that principal and teacher incompetence is not the reason schools change little, with most of the changes that do occur being thrust upon them. There is little in the schooling culture to suggest that principals and teachers ought to become change agents and even less provision for helping them learn how to do so. Rather, the expectation of reform is that our schools simply do better at what they are already doing.

We deliberately closed down the League as an organization, leaving the districts and their participating schools to do what they would do. In subsequent visits to southern California, I nearly always encountered "veterans" who spoke of those "golden years." If the schools slowly returned to what they had been, were the 6 years worthwhile nonetheless?

The League of Cooperating Schools initiative taught me about the layers of perceptions and understanding of schools, and particularly the schooling enterprise—from the symbols to the deep structures. Any one of these is seen differently by students, teachers, administrators, school board members, policymakers, corporate leaders, and, of course, parents. And there is a reality that shapes these perceptions and understandings. I do not remember why I decided next to find and study these realities deeply. Let me simply say that a dozen philanthropic foundations and agencies thought the inquiry important enough to fund. I am deeply appreciative. What became the Study of Schooling in the United States was launched.

As I remember it, I developed no detailed proposal, only the framing of an idea. I do remember that I wrote for members of my team a memorandum—eight pages, I think. Each staff member, some of whom had participated in the League of Cooperating Schools initiative, received a copy as I invited him or her to join us. And then I met with the group and suggested that we imagine a ship from outer space hovering over a school, with its occupants wondering about the big yellow bugs below and the little bugs coming out of them. Then the spaceship would land and the visitors would ask many questions. What might they ask about what they saw and what would we tell them? The study was begun.

Our small advisory board consisted of only five people, representative of different fields of study, all of whom had broken out of these fields to address larger domains of human endeavor. When we got at last to issues of methodology, "thick description" emerged without competition. Our descriptions and analyses of what we did, struggled with, and found are detailed elsewhere.[11] I report here only a few things that appear to me particularly relevant to the themes of this chapter.

Among my many learnings from the study is that the more complex and layered the phenomena studied, the greater the need for thick descriptions and the more likely the finding of core problems. And the finding of core problems creates the greater likelihood of finding powerful hypotheses regarding the fixing of these problems.

Partway through the study, findings were piling up so consistently that it was impossible to escape thinking about strategies for addressing the issues and problems of schooling. The problems were of such magnitude that the prospect of principals' and teachers' alone being able to solve them became a mirage. As with preceding work, nowhere did we find stewards of a school who had a clear purpose, let alone a public one shared with parents. The link between parents and their schools was fragile, consisting mostly of information, which many parents viewed as insufficient. Curricula, instructional matters, and staff development were district driven, not school driven. The circumstances necessary for ordinary people to do extraordinary things are simply not part of our schooling enterprise.

One afternoon during our Study of Schooling, sitting in the tranquility of my UES office, I toyed with the idea of a hypothetical bridge that was anchored at one end in the school yard, rising over the traffic of Sunset Boulevard, and anchored in the turf beyond, across which would travel a steady stream of university colleagues heading for nearby schools and another stream of elementary and secondary school colleagues coming to the UCLA campus in a partnership of mutual renewal. Out of sharing such thoughts with Paul Heckman and Ken Sirotnik, a couple of close colleagues, the Southern California School–University Partnership was created, funded by the Mott Foundation.

The journeys across the bridge did not materialize, but the partnership among the school districts got off to a good start anyway. At about that time, I told Chancellor Charles Young that 16 years in the deanship was more than I had anticipated and perhaps more than enough. And, without talking about it very much, Lynn and I decided that it was time to get closer to our roots. Being out of employment was relaxing, and we enjoyed watching our new floating home being built over a muddy lot that was several fathoms below the surface of Lake Union in Seattle. And then came another of those unsolicited invitations, and I was suddenly a professor at the University of Washington. Every now and then, it crosses my mind that my first teaching position, in Surrey, is the only job I ever applied for.

With a 5-year grant from the Exxon Education Foundation and another from the Mertz-Gilmore Foundation in hand, the Center for Educational Renewal came into being, and I set out to put together a small team once more. Ken Sirotnik, who had been a pivotal figure in the Study of Schooling, left Los Angeles and joined me. We did not need to persuade Roger Soder, who with Richard Andrews was winding up a study of the Seattle schools, to join us. We soon were into a comprehensive study of educator preparation programs in colleges and universities of a sample of settings in the several census areas of the United States.

Our previous studies had resulted in our posing some predictive hypotheses about what we would find, hypotheses that were repeatedly supported by the consistency of our findings. Were it not for wanting to strengthen our new study with more data, we might well have ceased our inquiry after simply adding the data from visiting only a dozen settings to the data gathered by other means. As anticipated, we found little evidence of principals' and teachers' being prepared to make their future schools into renewing institutions. Programs were oriented almost exclusively to instructional child care. The necessary integration of the three groups playing some part in every program we studied— colleges of education, departments in the arts and sciences, and schools providing student teaching—was missing. Indeed, they rarely engaged in planning or conducting together any part of the whole. There was neither a shared purpose for the education of educators nor collaborative curricular provisions for addressing the important questions of what the schools in which future teachers would teach are for and what they were doing.

I took seriously John Dewey's view that educational research should arise out of practice and the results returned to practitioners.[12] Toward the end of writing *A Place Called School,* my report of the Study of Schooling, my thoughts turned frequently to the realization that educators and others engaged with our schools deserved more than thick descriptions of them and their context from which problems and needs might readily become apparent.[13] *A Place Called School* provided a good deal of this, and it also made clear, I thought, that the surrounding infrastructure lacked the conditions for supporting renewal of our schools. There should not be an accompanying blueprint, but rather a guiding agenda developed collaboratively by policymakers, educators, and local communities.

I brought with me to Seattle an announced commitment to create a network of school–university partnerships for educational renewal. In spring 1986, *Education Week* announced our creation, through the Center for Educational Renewal, of a national network of 10 member settings. I had prepared a document, first presented at an annual meeting of the Council of Chief State School Officers. Following some adjustments, it became the agenda that, we thought, the 10 embryonic school–university partnerships had studied carefully and agreed to be guided by. We were wrong; some had, but some had not. Some of the university representatives were, shall we say, testy about their institutions' and their school partners' having equal power and status. When the question "whose agenda is this anyway?" was asked, we knew that we needed to abandon our plans or seek a fresh iteration of them. We closed down the first iteration and spread the word that we would try for a second iteration in 18 months, for which they might apply if they wished. The intervening time would require their thorough exploration of the criteria for admission to the network.

The work of developing a new, more comprehensive, and more detailed agenda was begun, as was a collaboration with the American Association of Colleges for Teacher Education and the Education Commission of the

States for engaging state leaders and educators in conversations about our plans. One of the three books that reported our Study of the Education of Educators included 19 postulates—"reasonable" propositions—regarding conditions necessary for the development of robust teacher education programs and, therefore, robust school-university partnerships.[14] We released the word that we were ready to take applications for membership in what became the National Network for Educational Renewal (NNER).

We were overwhelmed with expressions of interest from a quarter of the teacher-preparation institutions in the United States. We created a selection process that gave us a cohort of eight entirely new settings and several more from the first cohort, followed by a slow addition of others. In 1992, we created the nonprofit Institute for Educational Inquiry (IEI), which became, among other things, the home of the NNER.

Today, this network is an independent agency embracing 24 school-university partnerships in 20 states and 1 Canadian province, more than 100 school districts, 42 institutions of higher education, and countless schools. Since its founding, the primary intellectual endeavor of the IEI has been the unpacking and clarification of what we named in the early 1990s the Agenda for Education in a Democracy. Since then, a steady stream of books and papers, speeches, conferences, and workshops has advanced awareness and implementation of the Agenda.

We know, of course, that educators require partners in renewing our schools and especially the schooling enterprise. Not just schools and universities but also the other two major subcultures of this enterprise—policymakers and communities—must join in the public purpose of schooling: the education of a democratic people. When my colleagues and I speak of this purpose, we are addressing the necessity of everyone's taking care of a democracy that, presumably, is of, by, and for the people and the necessity of educating everyone to assume and fulfill this responsibility.

When we say and write that our Agenda for Education in a Democracy is nonnegotiable, we mean that it is not open for revision into nondemocratic alternatives. There are quite different conditions to be put in place when addressing, say, the education of homecare workers rather than preschool teachers. But they, too, must be prepared to take good care of our democracy. As I say to educators who question the nonnegotiability of our Agenda, "May a thousand flowers bloom."

The opening chapter of our most recent book, *Education and the Making of a Democratic People,* begins as follows:

> On Friday, December 1, 2006, the editorial column of a Seattle newspaper began with the following sentence: "Whatever became of the idea that representative democracy is the essential starting point for public education?" One might also ask the question, "Whatever happened to the idea that public education is the essential starting point for addressing the well-being of democracy?"[15]

Getting the latter question firmly established in the public domain is the work in which the NNER and the IEI are now increasingly engaged. The challenge is to return discourse and action to the local communities and for them to join with the other subcultures of schooling in the making of a democratic people.

·‿

When did the roots of caring deeply about the relationship between education and democracy first lodge themselves in the ecosystem of my mind? I do not know. But I do know when I first became deeply involved with it. Serendipity was the major drummer one more time. I think it was early in the academic year before the Goodlad family departed Chicago for the West Coast that a stranger named Gerhard Hirschfeld knocked on my office door.

He came to talk with me about a small group of extraordinary scholars he had brought together, one by one, into a conclave named the Council for the Study of Mankind. Perhaps it was because it was an all-male group that the last word was not "humankind." Sustaining the male vocabulary, his concern was with man's inhumanity to man. World War II had ripped his family apart. What could he do to help right the world? Organizing the group was a beginning; he was devoting his modest resources to it. Would I be interested in joining? I was.

The group was awesome. All had far-flung reputations, and I had read some of the work of several. Our conversations led to the writing and publication of several books from a mankind perspective. I carried my involvement with me to California, where new colleagues and I advanced the theme in the UES and wrote a book about it. More and more I came to realize that democracy is, as yet, the best way of life for humankind. Hence, its care through the education of a democratic public is a nonnegotiable agenda. It is the most challenging agenda humankind has ever faced.

Dee Hock, to whom I referred earlier and who took the lead in founding VISA, one of the largest enterprises on earth, writes the following in the prologue of his book, *Birth of the Chaordic Age:*

> We are living on the knife's edge of one of those rare and momentous turning points in human history. . . . Our current forms of organization are almost universally based on compelled behavior—on tyranny, for that is what compelled behavior is, no matter how benign it may appear or how carefully disguised and exercised. The organization of the future will be the embodiment of *community* based on *shared purpose* calling to the *higher aspirations of people.*[16]

I am beyond the number of pages in this book allotted to me and so must bring my story to an end. Nearly 7 decades have passed since I walked through the drizzle toward the front stoop of Woodward Hill School and the children huddled together there. It has been a great journey. I would like to start out all over again, but with my present ecology of educative belief and with those wonderful colleagues who made up that succession of creative teams, and the necessary new ones who would join us. But with the partner who was by my side for 6 of those decades no longer there, it would be necessary to decline the opportunity.

Notes

1. Goodlad, J. I. (2004). *Romances with schools: A life of education.* New York: McGraw-Hill.

2. For the power of this nonschool educating, see Martin, J. R. (2007). *Educational metamorphoses: Philosophical reflections on identity and culture.* Lanham, MD: Rowman & Littlefield.

3. Fenstermacher, G. D (2008). In search of agency for classroom teachers. In L. J. Waks (Ed.), *Leaders in philosophy of education: Intellectual self portraits.* Rotterdam, The Netherlands: Sense Publishers.

4. Postman, N., & Weingartner, C. (1969). *Teaching as a subversive activity.* New York: Delacorte Press.

5. Sarason, S. B. (1996). *Revisiting "The culture of the school and the problem of change."* New York: Teachers College Press.

6. Goodlad, J. I. (1949). Some effects of promotion and nonpromotion upon the social and personal adjustment of children. Ph.D. dissertation, University of Chicago.

7. Hock, D. (1999). *Birth of the chaordic age* (p. 192). San Francisco: Berrett-Kohler.

8. Goodlad, J. I., & Anderson, R. H. (1959). *The nongraded elementary school.* New York: Harcourt Brace. (Original work published 1959; second edition published 1963; revised edition published 1987 by Teachers College Press)

9. Hock, D. (1999). *Birth of the chaordic age* (p. 117). San Francisco: Berrett-Kohler.

10. Goodlad, J. I., Klein, M. F., & Associates. (1974). *Looking behind the classroom door* (pp. 12–18). Worthington, OH: Charles A. Jones.

11. Goodlad, J. I. (1984). *A place called school.* New York: McGraw-Hill. (Original work published 1984; 20th anniversary edition published 2004)

12. See Dewey, J. (1929). *The sources of a science of education.* New York: Horace Liveright.

13. Goodlad, J. I. (1984). *A place called school.* New York: McGraw-Hill. (Original work published 1984; 20th anniversary edition published 2004)

14. Goodlad, J. I. (1990). *Teachers for our nation's schools.* San Francisco: Jossey-Bass.

15. Goodlad, J. I., Soder, R., & McDaniel, B. (Eds.). (2008). *Education and the making of a democratic people* (p. 9). Boulder, CO: Paradigm.

16. Hock, D. (1999). *Birth of the chaordic age* (pp. 5–6). San Francisco: Berrett-Kohler.

Circa 1965.
As Dean of
the Harvard
Graduate School
of Education.

Circa 1995.
In Birmingham,
England, visiting
schools while
on Coalition of
Essential Schools
business.

Circa 2002.
With his
granddaughter
Nancy.

Theodore R. Sizer

·◞

Lessons Learned

Theodore R. Sizer was born and raised in the town of Bethany, CT. He attended Pomfret School in eastern Connecticut and graduated from Yale College in 1953. He served on active duty in Germany in the Ninth Infantry Division of the U.S. Army. Upon returning to the United States, he taught at the Roxbury Latin School in Boston, followed by a year as a Master at the Melbourne Church of England Grammar School in Australia.

Upon his return from Australia, he enrolled at Harvard University, earning an M.A. in Teaching followed by a Ph.D. in American History and Education. Ted worked at the Harvard Graduate School of Education from 1956 to 1972 and served as its Dean from 1964 through 1972. He then returned to school teaching as an instructor in History and Headmaster at Phillips Academy in Andover, MA.

In 1981, he returned to research to lead "A Study of High Schools," a national inquiry into American secondary education. In 1984, he moved to Brown University as Professor of Education and founded the Coalition of Essential Schools, now a nationwide association of more than 1,000 reform-minded schools. In 1997, he retired from Brown as University Professor Emeritus. Sizer has written several books on American secondary education, the best known being the Horace trilogy: *Horace's Compromise, Horace's School,* and *Horace's Hope.* In 1998–99, he and his wife Nancy served as the acting co-principals of the Francis W. Parker Charter Essential School in Devens, MA. They also taught a course on secondary school design at Harvard University from 1997 to 2006. In 1999, the Sizers authored *The Students Are Watching: Schools and the Moral Contract.* In 2004, Nancy, Ted, and Deborah Meier issued *Keeping School: Letters to Parents,* which emerged from the Sizers' work at Parker and Meier's work at the Central Park East Secondary School in New York.

Ted taught for 3 years at Brandeis University, and he and Nancy took part in the Spencer Seminary there for several years. They have four children and ten grandchildren and reside in the small town of Harvard, MA.

•⤳

To give "lessons" that I have learned to the "next generation" is, alas, an act of arrogance. Who am I to lecture the young? Nonetheless, it is one that is appealing to an elder, a retired educator. My advice might serve as an explanation of what I did as a school person in the past, but that is the stuff of history. Times change, and with that change the ways and means of living, teaching, and learning alter. Still, if youth wants to read modern history, my story might help.

In contrast with my teenaged years, today's secondary school students are bombarded by the media, almost all of which is produced by for-profit companies—a great 21st-century bazaar. "If it sells, it must be good" is the rule of thumb today. In the 1930s and 1940s, when I was growing up, we had the radio and the newspaper. Today's young have Palm Pilots, cell phones, and all sorts of recording and listening devices. These not-so-youngsters connect with one another at all times during the day and, to the sorrow of parents, at night. They also connect with the offerings of the modern media continually. These all-too-unwary adolescents are a large and soft market. It's a new, fascinating, and troubling world.

All that said, what follows is my story, my professional *cursus honorum*. (Of course, few kids today study Latin. However, some may figure out what that *cursus* and *honorum* might mean and have a chuckle about how an old fuddy duddy spent his working years.)

My Early Career in the Military

Some careers start when one is very young. Mine certainly did. I was lucky with the family I was born into. I was my parents' sixth child, their youngest and the only boy. My father was a Professor of the History of Art and Director of the Art Gallery at Yale University. He was a busy man, and he was fortunate that my mother skillfully ruled our house in the (then) rural town of Bethany, some dozen miles north of New Haven, Connecticut.

At the advent of World War II—on December 8th, 1941, the day after the Day of Infamy, as President Roosevelt called it—my father re-enlisted in the Army. He had served briefly during the World War I but had never been sent overseas. The Army now placed him in the Arts and Monuments section of military government. They briefly trained him at the University of Virginia and then sent him straightaway to Morocco and thence to Tunisia. There, he started negotiations with his German and Italian counterparts (usually in the no-man's land between the two armies) to determine how both the Allied and Axis armies could steer clear of early arts monuments in that theater, a remarkable instance of restraint between warring factions.

The Allies soon carried the battle north to Sicily and then into mainland Italy. Meetings of the arts representatives continued between the battle lines (literally), and these were often livened up with a bottle of Chianti wine shared by the (supposed) enemies. The negotiators' most regretted failure was the destruction of the great, ancient library at Monte Cassino; their greatest success was the protection of Rome (by pre-agreement, the armies simply went around that ancient capitol city).

Dad was then sent north to England, but while in preparation for the cross-Channel invasion, he suffered a stroke. He was sent home to a Veterans Administration hospital and thence back to our house in Bethany. He "worked" during his disability by hooking rugs, a skill which he chose because it addressed his infirmity—semi-paralyzed hands that often painfully tingled and became stone cold—and thereby speeded his recovery. His rugs, some 200 over the years, were always designed to be given as presents to important friends and family members, and they are stunning pieces of art. In due course, he completely regained his health and returned to his Yale classroom. I, as an undergraduate at Yale, audited his lectures and traveled with him and a group of his students to New York, where he marched us around the great treasures of the Metropolitan Museum of Art, lecturing as he strode.

In the martial tradition of my family, I enrolled in Yale's Reserve Officers' Training Corps (ROTC) program and spent one summer in full-time training at Fort Sill in Oklahoma. This was followed by my assignment to the Ninth Infantry Division in Germany. I served in one of its artillery battalions barracked in Schwäbisch Gmünd and, later, at a Non-Commissioned Officers' (NCO) Training School in Schwabach, a small town near Nürnberg. I learned much about teaching from these assignments. My "students" were mostly in their late teens and male, high-school graduates or dropouts. Still, having a sergeant stationed in the back of the classroom meant that I didn't need to worry much about classroom management.

I engaged the family military tradition further while teaching at the Melbourne Church of England Grammar School in Australia. There, in my American uniform and with the blessing of my U.S. Army Australian Command, I served in that old school's Cadet Corps. I "commanded" a company of students and took them for spring vacation to Puckapunyal, the Australian army's equivalent of our Fort Benning. Even as late as 1958, the Aussies were still afraid of a resurgent Japan, and, in time, a newly focused and powerful China. (Vietnam was not yet on their diplomatic screen.) Back home, I continued active Reserve duty with a unit based at Fort Devens. In time, I resigned in disgust: This "Reservist" show was a wasteful game, fun for pay.

Lesson Learned? As a citizen in a democracy, one has to pull his or her appropriate weight. At the least, this means voting in all elections; taking some part in local government; speaking out when speech is necessary; and exercising restraint in word and action, which is one of the key requirements of collective, civilized government (including with regards to decisions about whether or not to go to war, a lesson our current generation of national leaders appears to have forgotten).

The essence of restraint is humility, the acceptance of the fact that no one among us has all the answers. Service in the military is just a small piece of this—or a large part, if your unit is called to fight in Iraq. Loyalty, duty, restraint, honest criticism—*humility*—when such criticism is due: These are worthy virtues.

A citizen today, with America being unnecessarily entangled in politics in Iraq, surely wishes that (among other things) his or her national government would exhibit at least some measure of humility. Some politicians appear to believe that if *they* say it, it must be correct. Only rarely is there an "on the other hand" attitude expressed; indeed, its very expression is all too often considered a sort of treason.

Anne-Liese Wellershaus and World War II

As a young child I saw another, more painful side of duty. During the 1930s, when my parents dragged their five daughters (I had yet to arrive), on a trip to Europe to visit art galleries, they engaged a young German woman, Anne-Liese Wellershaus, to accompany them as an *au pair*. She continued this work in Bethany when I was born but went back to Germany when I started school. It was soon apparent that this young woman was a committed anti-Nazi, and when the Fascist machine started rolling in 1940, my parents offered her asylum and a room in our family home in Connecticut. They arranged a job for her as an aide in the kindergarten and 1st-grade classes at the Foote School, a progressive K–8 elementary school in New Haven that my mother had helped launch and which was led, ironically, by an English refugee from the Nazi bombings of England. "Anni," as we kids called her, also started an egg business, with her chickens scratching around our barnyard. My youngest sister, Alice, and I quickly attached ourselves to her. We helped her prepare her "reports" to the parents of her Foote School students, as her written English was not strong. Only later did we recognize that, in the substantive sense, we had "two mothers."

After World War II, in 1970, she was lured back to Germany by an offer of marriage from a man who had, to put it bluntly, jilted her in the 1930s. Werner Vowinckel had been a German soldier in the war and kept a large portrait of Hitler behind the shower curtain in their apartment. It was there that my wife and I discovered it when we visited the Vowinckels soon after their marriage. We have wondered often about what Anni thought about the picture, but it was a subject that we never dared to broach with her.

Lesson Learned? People can and do live with contradictory values—for instance, marriage vows versus commitments to freedom and democracy—and this may not at all be a display of two-facedness. Rather, it is a stark expression of what life often thrusts upon us.

My Graduate School Years

I arrived in 1957 at the Harvard Graduate School of Arts and Sciences, initially as a candidate for the Master of Arts in Teaching program and later as a Ph.D. candidate in History and Education. I learned a batch of lessons there—which is, of course, one of the main reasons one goes into post-baccalaureate schooling. As a condition of my admission, I was required to take a fistful of History and Social Sciences courses to make up for my "deficiency" of having majored in English. (History Departments, at least the one at Harvard, usually took a dim view of studies taken beyond their immediate purview.) My advisor, Bernard Bailyn, urged me to concentrate on late 19th-century America, drawing on the university's strong manuscript collection from that period. I soon found myself below ground level in the university archives, delving into the Charles William Eliot papers. Eliot was, especially for his time, a national figure. Fortunately, he (or his secretary) also was a pack rat. He served as Chairman of the so-called Committee of Ten of the National Educational Association (now known as the National Education Association).

The Committee of Ten settled on what its members called the "main line subjects" of English, mathematics, history and the social sciences, science (Chemistry, Physics, Biology), and the arts. Eliot committed himself to selling the Committee's recommendations, and he traveled widely (no mean feat back in his day; all that travel was by way of unreliable rail). Astonishingly, the effort worked. Today's schools, over a century later, reflect these "core" subjects. Their significance is accepted as a matter of course, almost as if they were a truth delivered from on high, and is rarely challenged. (Eliot would have liked that "on high" bit.)

Lesson Learned? One of America's most important and richest historical traditions is the demanding curricular core of middle and high school courses represented by English, the arts, mathematics, history/social studies, science, and the several vocational subjects. I had been confronted with these disciplines in my schooling career at Foote School and Pomfret School—both self-proclaimed "progressive" schools that believed themselves to be on the cutting edge but that were, in fact, unthinking copiers of the 1890s.

The late 19th-century Committee of Ten classification of "core subjects" has today an almost totally unchallenged grip on the profession's—and the public's—thinking about what high school should be about. Since the Committee issued its report, there have been a swarm of well-meaning scholarly and professional groups built around these subjects to support the in-school labors of teachers. Also, our state and federal programs and laws reflect the perceived "sanctity" of these categories and are so deeply entrenched in this line of thinking that few—even among education scholars, who might be expected to be more reserved and analytic in their judgments—contemplate any change. Indeed, to do so would provoke a barrage of criticism and the skepticism of faculty committees that oversee promotion and tenure. Our professional blindness is an embarrassment.

My Deanship at the
Harvard Graduate School of Education

Between 1964 and 1972, as Dean of the Harvard Graduate School of Education, I was both helped and challenged by the outside world. I was helped by the attention that was being given to education, especially with regard to educating a wider spectrum of children than had been recognized in the Sputnik era. This coincided with my own feeling that Schools of Education should take part in furthering social justice through the reforms and improvements which seemed possible in the early Johnson years. The passage of generous laws, especially the Elementary and Secondary Act of 1965, signified Congress's commitment to the nation's poorest and least advantaged children.

With the help of those laws, Harvard's School of Education was able to hire people of broad clinical and scholarly experience in cities. Our recruiting for students of color grew more effective, especially when we sent our students out on the road with the admissions officers and when there were federal scholarships available to people who had broad experience in and commitment to the field of education, but who could benefit from more years of study.

The challenge came when the bitterness of the late 1960s began to undermine the feeling that Whites could contribute to the schooling of poor Blacks. Richard Nixon's presidency further weakened the support that the nation was prepared to give. A sudden retrenchment in funds hit all universities hard, especially those that were working on large and carefully-constructed research projects in cities.

Student unrest, much of which arose from resistance to the draft and to the conduct of the Vietnam War, also slowed down our urban agenda somewhat. The situation grew confusing, and then hostile, at least in some quarters. There are no heroes from the late 1960s, at least in academia. My most vigilant efforts were just to keep the boat steady, not to sail it fast or in exactly the right direction.

Lessons Learned? The sense that education—and more schooling—was the most likely vehicle to address the nation's pockets of poverty and racism.

I learned much about persistence from the willingness of many young adults to work hard for as long as it took them to receive a master's or doctorate degree without fear of mockery. ("What's that old guy doing in my graduate school classes?")

Also, I came to understand that even stuffy old universities can change, if they have stable and effective leadership (as was the case in my Harvard years, when the stubborn and principled Nathan Marsh Pusey was its president). Indeed, universities should "change" as the shape and substance of the scholarly disciplines change. Stubborn universities have no place in academic life.

Phillips Academy

Between 1972 and 1981, I was the Headmaster of Phillips Academy in Andover, Massachusetts. Although the setting was much more bucolic and traditional than the wide reach of Harvard's Graduate School of Education, these were years of living among teenagers—my own children included—and in, by American standards, an ancient institution. It has survived and thrived because it shifted with the times, its leaders sorting out which "changes" led into cul-de-sacs and which were timely and substantively defensible.

I was drawn to the school partly by its Charter, a remarkably eloquent document that I had studied as a graduate student. In 1778, in the midst of the American Revolution, Phillips's founders had vowed to provide a school for "youth from every quarter," the rich and the poor, the pious or the religiously unconvinced. Now, in 1972, the trustees were ready to include girls under the title of "youth," a decision that enraged some senior faculty and alumni. Most of the rest of the faculty agreed with the decision of the trustees, and I was asked to get it done.

We were fortunate that Abbot Academy—a school for girls that was founded just 50 years later than Phillips and by members of the same extended family—was contiguous. The two schools had increased their academic and social contacts in previous years. Some of the Abbot trustees and alumni were as stubbornly protective of its character as a school for females as some of the Phillips folk were about their "all male" school. Nonetheless, the fact could not be hidden that the differences in their endowments were substantial. Phillips was rich, and Abbot was poor.

The easy part turned out to be the initial negotiations, which were realistic and polite. More challenging was the merger of two proud institutions of somewhat different character and practices. This sort of log jam was familiar to many in academic life. As my father had inscribed on one of the rugs he hooked, "Marriage makes two one, but which one?"

Our answer had to be "both," not an easy answer in those tense, black-or-white times. However, over the years it became clear that we were creating a new Andover, one whose characteristics, practices, and people came from both the old school and from the newcomers whom we welcomed into our work.

Access to Andover didn't end with girls and women, however. We began to work on recruiting students from all income levels and racial and religious groups throughout the nation and the world. Our goal was a school that was vibrant and interesting because of its diversity. Our extensive scholarship programs helped us to begin the long climb to recruiting on a "needs-blind" basis. *Youth from every Quarter* indeed. At the same time, I learned much from my veteran colleague teachers about how to adapt serious work so that it "fits" each student without losing its intent and rigor.

Lessons Learned? Even a (frankly) stuffy, 200-year-old school can reshape itself with concerted trustee and faculty action. Entrenched tradition should not be a barrier to reform, whether in private or public sectors. A sensible merger of two institutions can be more than the mere gathering of its two parts.

Also, students can be promoted on the basis of their demonstrated performance, which limits the humiliation of those students who take longer than 4 years to complete their studies.

Furthermore, in such a school, there is room for students from abroad—Europe, Asia, Africa—on a respected basis, even though their customs, diets, and religions vary.

Moreover, such an old, fiercely partisan, religious school (adhering to the starchiest form of Calvinism in its founding years) can accommodate students and faculty members of all faiths and provide common worship services involving different traditions.

Finally, that adolescents are ready and willing—and often proud—to do the scut work of every such institution, such as dishwashing, snow shoveling, floor sweeping and scrubbing, and more, under the close direction of staff members who themselves come from varied "quarters," some of whom may not speak much English.

Horace's Compromise and the Coalition of Essential Schools

By the early 1980s, I found that my biggest questions—questions begging confrontation—no longer concerned Andover. Instead, they involved the malaise I sensed in other high schools in the United States. With three children still in college and one in graduate school, I took the big plunge into research. As one of my mentors scolded, I "took a big lead off first without knowing where second was." Today, we would probably call it a midlife crisis.

No matter; it worked out. With help from some generous foundations, I was able to finance a reasonably large study over 4 years. It had three distinct but overlapping parts: my own years of travel, research, and writing, which became the foundation for my book *Horace's Compromise: The Dilemma of the American High School* (1985); a deeper study of 12 high schools in different parts of the country, which was published in *The Shopping Mall High School* by Arthur G. Powell, Eleanor Farrar, and David K. Cohen (1986); and a history of high schools in the United States since 1945 written by Robert Hampel and titled *The Last Little Citadel* (1986).

The story we told was a disappointing one for us all, full of challenges for educators and citizens. However the new ways of doing research, which involved our sharing of fieldnotes and drafts, and the resulting discussions that came from our collaboration were heady indeed. Each book was influenced by the others in the group, and much of my work since that time has been based on the insights I gained during those years.

By the end of those "full-time research" years, I prepared to take up my post as a professor and chairman of the Department of Education at Brown. I pondered what I thought we had learned. Happily, I now had the vigorous support of Brown University's then-President, Howard Swearer. Moreover, the foundations that had funded our studies of what we were convinced were serious flaws in the design and functioning of high schools now expected us to make a serious effort to improve them. From that came the Coalition of Essential Schools, along with the financing to launch it.

The name we chose is instructive.

A "Coalition" was necessary, as we were convinced that each admirable high school had its own characteristics and its own integrity and should not be dependent on others for the specifics of its design. It would be responsive most of all to its own people, in its own community, to design the kinds of curricula and assessments most likely to lead to success.

It was "Essential" because we believed that schools had to strip down their offerings to concentrate on the content and skills that were the most crucial in helping children to learn to use their minds well.

All other benefits of schooling—and there are many—would need to be secondary to that primary goal. Our commitment to "schools" was deliberate as we believed that they were the most effective and appropriate way to reach children.

Nonetheless we asked ourselves: Did a collection of autonomous schools really need some kind of "Coalition," after all? Couldn't they flourish in isolation, without pressure to make them adapt to the character of other places?

To address this issue, I decided to try and give our movement more shape in the form of a set of "Common Principles" that reflected the kinds of changes we sought to make. These axioms had to do with knowing children well, promoting them on the basis of their performance, and valuing depth over breadth in learning. While they were largely general in nature, they had to be taken seriously; each would require difficult, specific practices that reflected their commitments. That done, I set about searching for school colleagues who could help me to flesh the Common Principles out. I hoped to find perhaps a dozen of such colleagues in varied schools.

Helped again by foundations, the number of participating schools grew, and as each new school was added to our group, there was new excitement—and new challenges. Unlike any job I had ever had before, we were on completely new ground. And like other "start-ups" with which I have been involved since—especially the Francis W. Parker Charter Essential School in Devens, Massachusetts—there was something to learn and decisions to be made every day.

The task fundamentally depended on gathering people who wished to work within one reform framework. Brave pioneers among the earliest principals in the group, such as Deborah Meier and Dennis Littky, are still colleagues and soulmates of mine decades later. Other fine people came and, for one reason or another (usually retirement and the hiring of district superintendents who wanted their own "signature" reforms), left. Nonetheless, our Education Department at Brown was full of experience, talent, energy, and good will.

Institutional policy questions abounded:

- How big did we want to be? When does scale make a reform effort stagnant and rigid?
- Should a school pay to join us, or should we pay it? Who was getting the benefit? (We decide we are all benefiting and chose to leave money out of the process.)
- In what ways could we learn from these schools? How could we at Brown help them? How could we document their successes in a form that was helpful to other schools?
- If a school changed, should it stay in the Coalition? How could we honor their autonomy and at the same time create a productive community?
- In what ways should we allow our donors help us to evolve our practice? Should money drive our priorities?

What we learned was that these were sensible, indeed, crucially important, questions.

As the Coalition deepened its roots and stabilized its work, another question—again driven by money—was posed: Could we, and others, learn from an alliance of kindred groups that shared our general ends but that used different means? What sort of alliance was practically possible if our associated schools depended on the scores from standardized tests to signify their performance?

Over time, we differed with some other national school reform efforts, such as ones which, in our view, focused disproportionately on testing. We worked successfully, however, with Harvard Professor Howard Gardner's "Project Zero" enterprise, which dealt primarily with arts education; Dr. James Comer's Yale-based School Development Project; and the Education Development Center in Newton, Massachusetts, led by Janet Whitla, which had a wide portfolio of school reform enterprises under way. Together we brought our ideas together in the so-called ATLAS Communities Project and took them to communities as diverse as Norfolk, Virginia, and Southern Maine. We grew more interested in national educational policy, feeling that we could help the teachers in our schools more if we influenced both the media and the politicians who were determining the environment in which they worked.

After I retired, the Coalition's national office moved out of a university and to Oakland, California, where it faces some of the same challenges it struggled with when I was involved as well as some new ones. The Coalition is made up of regions, which better allow teachers to get together often to share what have proven to be good ideas—at least in one school. More schools are "mentoring" other schools in more formal ways. And the annual gathering of the faithful, the Fall Forum, is still one of the highlights of my year. It's not just that I see old friends; when I'm at the Forum, I learn so much about what I still want to know.

Lessons Learned? First, that an idea, or *ideas,* can drive reform and the practice that reflects that reform. One does not need specific "practices" that are to be learned and "put into place" (in unlovely contemporary jargon).

Second, that there is both joy and challenge in this sort of effort to knock off some of the professional barnacles that all of us professionals inevitably get. ("This is what we do. We must do it. If we do not do it, we will jeopardize our jobs and may tangle with our union contract.")

Third, that there can never be a permanent "pure" design of a school (or school system). All must be in movement, gathering the best of emerging experience and new research findings.

Fourth, that strong organizations can ally with other such enterprises sharing common commitments.

The Annenberg Challenge

In 1993, the awe of the Annenberg Challenge, which Brown's President Vartan Gregorian (Greg) and I discovered, was only a glint in Walter Annenberg's eye. At a meeting at the Annenberg home in St David's, Pennsylvania, Walter made a boldly generous financial suggestion. His wife gently urged him to increase it—substantially. Greg and I blinked and just sat there, working to keep poker faces. In but a moment, Walter suggested a major figure, one which would allow Brown to create a free-standing academic Institute to work with worthy nonprofit, grant-making institutions in getting the best total return on their initial investment. The ultimate figure was in several multiples of millions. After lunch, Greg and I returned from St. David's to the Philadelphia airport, each ordered a beer and a sandwich, and two bunches of flowers for our wives, who had been forced to live with our "Annenberg" fantasies for so many distracting weeks.

Then came the hard part: What were we going to do with all that money? How could we develop a plan that would be focused on the children who needed it most—at the insistence of the Ambassador—and that would be progressive in its pedagogy and assessment, sensitive to the context of the cities and the schools it worked with, and yet that would be coherent and would ensure that the impact of the grant would be understood as a mission—more than just the chance to get money?

This required reconnecting with every trusted personal contact I had made in my years of working to build the Coalition. We needed allies, not competitors, yet it couldn't be considered to be "Ted's money." The announcement would be made at the White House, but this was to be kept secret. Our plan had to be impressive enough to survive grilling by the White House press corps on that day.

We decided to give the grant to several large cities, and we picked a few which would be able to use the money well. The night before the announcement was to be made, I learned that the Ambassador wanted there to be matching grants in each of the cities that received Annenberg dollars. I could understand his reasoning: Walter wanted whole communities to "get on the bandwagon" of improving schools for their most needy children. In raising money for matching grants, cities would not only spend more than only Annenberg funds on a worthy project but would have to engage the talents and passions of a wide variety of people. Yet I worried—and rightly so—that the richer, more organized cities would have an advantage over the others, and that they would present plans which, however sensible, might not be imaginative enough to overcome the tremendous odds we faced.

Lesson Learned: Lightning can always strike.

The Francis W. Parker
Charter Essential School

The 1993 Massachusetts Education Reform Act provided incentives for groups of citizens and educators to design and launch new public high schools, and a group of parents and retired educators (including ourselves) gathered on what had been the Fort Devens Army Base (at which, appropriately perhaps, I had served some years before when I was in the Army's Active Reserve) to design a new school. We came up with a design, the state approved it, and we opened our doors in an almost windowless army building designed for use by Army Intelligence units. (In fact, we found a map of East Germany pasted to a wall in the tomb-like basement level of the structure. We felt that we were helping the nation to recover from the Cold War and re-energize its children's education, all at the same time!)

We called our fledgling institution the Francis W. Parker Charter Essential School. Now housed in a more suitable structure, the old Devens Elementary School, Parker serves students in grades 7–12 with a sharply defined curriculum that is in play all 6 years consisting of mathematics/ science, arts/humanities, Spanish (the primary second language in our region of Massachusetts), and health (a strict state requirement). Students are "admitted" almost exclusively at the 7th-grade level on a blind lottery basis. (Actually the lottery takes families into consideration. If one member of a family gains admission through the lottery, his or her siblings are automatically admitted if they choose to apply.) Special needs students, save those with severe or unusual problems that are best addressed at a special school, are included in the applicant pool.

Most of Parker's students outperform what is expected of them. That is, their exhibited work, on the basis of faculty analysis and that of the state and visitors, exceeds what the state demands. This achievement is, of course, not perfect, and Parker has its share of distracted or lazy students. What is different for them, however, is that their distraction and laziness is known well by their advisors and most of the teachers. It is hard to hide at Parker.

As the reputation of the school has grown, we have created a "Teacher Center," now with its own building and program. It offers a variety of programs for visitors depending on their particular interests, and is the base for new programs that have emerged in our region, such as the New Teachers Collaborative (NTC). NTC participants hold jobs at schools in our region, and they come together at the Teacher Center for seminars and the opportunity to talk, a kind of "swap shop" for beginners.

While the NTC largely enrolls young persons right out of college or graduate school, it also includes older "career changers." The mix of young and old gives special spice to the seminars, most of which are based on a commonly read text. NTC students attend the CES Fall Forums, where they can learn from the experience of collaborative professional development.

Lessons Learned? That the concerted work of passionate and intelligent people can do much to add to the bare bones of a set of common principles. Parker's rubrics, advisories, projects, essential questions, and gateways reflect serious and joyous educational practice.

That creativity is extremely hard work, even when one's colleagues are like-minded in most respects, but that it is definitely worth it!

That teachers learn much by sharing their practice with people from other schools.

The Twin Cities Collaborative

In recent years, as a retired gentleman I have shown greater interest in my place as a citizen of central Massachusetts. The Twin Cities Collaborative (a not-for-profit entity based at Fitchburg State College in the politically and financially little-served small, industrial cities of Fitchburg and Leominster in central Massachusetts) came together in an effort to obtain grants that would give these towns' school systems long- and well-deserved prominence. At first, the districts' superintendents quickly planned to devote their efforts to matters of traditional interest, scattering the requested funds into political invisibility. This was a disappointment; but a new iteration of our collaboration was laid out, some earlier work in professional development was expanded, and we seem to be learning from our past experience.

The Fitchburg Art Museum, a small institution that owns a remarkable collection of paintings and prints, is creating, with the strong approval of the public school system's leaders, a small school-within-the-museum which allows students to connect the visual with the full range of subjects in their school curriculum. The "holding power" of this program—no dropouts—is unique in a district that is trying to cope with a flood of non-English speakers from South America.

Lesson Learned: Serious school reform takes time, and institutions such as schools do not stand still. If you want to help them, you have to engage them often enough that new staff members of the school believe that you are one of them, even if, technically, you are not.

Also, strong schools can be nested in unexpected places.

Coping with Illness

In recent years, I have continued to learn, this time about the nature and implications of my cancer. I had thought that all "medical problems" were dealt with solely on the basis of science: "This is the diagnosis; therefore, that must be the treatment." I have learned that, like schoolchildren, no two chemotherapy patients are quite alike. Diagnosis and the selection of the best potions to address cancer are more an art than a crisp science. My oncologist considered several approaches, checking each with colleagues, and as the infusions proceeded, made careful adjustments. The similarity with school teaching is direct and obvious.

Lesson Learned: Who is one's doctor matters, and his or her willingness to collaborate and to adjust the selected plan, even sharing decisions with the patient, matters too.

Lessons Learned by Looking Back

What CES and Parker represent is one sort of "reform" at the grassroots level that takes place at a particular time in a particular region. They embody some of best current practice. However, recent scholarship and writing suggests the need to look again at the provocative and useful work that is emerging.

A little known scholar, among professional educators at least, is the economist and political scientist Edward Banfield. His work on what he calls "social capital" goes back several decades. Banfield argues that social organizations—community—are crucial. At our best, humans are peace-loving and gregarious, and our institutions are—for the sake of convenience as well as out of necessity—*deliberate* communities: That is, they have an intended public purpose and duty.

Schools are, of course, surely the most, or one of the very most, universally accepted communities. Few educational administrators and public policy advocates, stuck in the grip of the past as though it were Gospel, have picked up on this line of thinking; indeed, many are not even aware of it.

What to do? We need to *read, write, and discuss more.* I have enjoyed writing since I was a young man, and have been grateful for the many "conversations" I have had with friends and strangers through the medium of my books. Such advice sounds both stale and obvious, but it is unquestionably needed.

We need to *never stop thinking*. A person has to keep at any subject or topic that clearly means a great deal to him or her. Politics, for example: One has to keep regular tabs on what his or her representative is doing. One has to take the time to visit that representative so that he or she has some sense of who you are. One has to follow the progress of a proposed law through the process at the Capitol or State House. One's representative has to know that you have a fair grasp of the details of what is being proposed.

Keep reading. Keep up with the news. Regularly read several newspapers and journals, as the topics chosen may present different points of view, from those of *The Washington Post, The New York Times,* the *Boston Herald,* and *The Nation.* Discuss what you read with others.

All healthy democracies depend on well informed and engaged citizens. Even as the candidates and representatives think in terms of pressure groups and conduct "focus groups" to detect the interests of those political blocs, just one citizen can make a difference. Her or his representative will know that an engaged citizen can readily be influential. Democracy is a one-by-one business. So, hang in there. One can make a difference in the political arena even if that "difference" seems small in contrast to affairs of state that have higher profiles. What is politically or educationally "hot" at any given moment may not be so even a few months later. Keep at it!

Circa 1977. Getting the results of his successful campaign to be elected to the school board of Champaign, Illinois. At 25 years old, he would become the youngest school board member in Illinois.

Circa 1992.
First year as principal of
Federal Hocking High School.

Circa 2004.
Hard at work at
Federal Hocking
High School.

George Wood

・ﾉ

Conclusion

George Wood is principal of Federal Hocking High School in Stewart, Ohio, and serves as the Executive Director of The Forum for Education and Democracy. Dr. Wood's 30-year career in public education includes work as a classroom teacher, school board member, professor of education, and school principal. He is the Founding Director of Wildwood Secondary School in Los Angeles and has served as principal of Federal Hocking High School for 16 years. Federal Hocking is a rural school in Appalachian Ohio which has been recognized as a Coalition of Essential Schools Mentor School, a First Amendment School, and as one of America's 100 Best by Readers' Digest. He authored Governor Ted Strickland's (OH) K-12 Education Transition Paper as well as the books *Schools That Work*, *Time to Learn*, and *Many Children Left Behind* (edited with Deborah Meier).

When Carl asked if I would write a "conclusion" to this collection, I readily agreed. I am starting to think I made a mistake.

The problem I have is how do I summarize the lessons we learn from Deborah Meier, Ted Sizer, Hank Levin, John Goodlad, and James Comer? Among them they have published hundreds of books and articles, they have led schools and school renewal networks, and they have touched the lives of thousands of educators and hundreds of thousands of children. And they have fought the good fight, refusing to give in to the pressure to adopt standards for the sake of standards; pushing against the bureaucratic or centralized control of schools, no matter how messy democratic, local control is; and trusting in the ability of teachers and parents to raise strong, thoughtful children in the face of enormous obstacles.

How does one summarize the lessons of these giants of education reform? I am writing this from my desk in the school where I am fortunate to be principal, Federal Hocking High School. It is quiet; school is out, summer is here, and the life seems to have been sucked out of the building. It is time for me and my staff to collect our energies again, plan for another year, and review what has been done and what has yet to be accomplished. As I walk around the school, I think about the influence these five luminaries have had on the lives of those of us who care about the future of America's public schools. Perhaps this is where I can find the temerity to try and summarize the lessons these leaders have for all of us.

A key theme that echoes through the stories of each of these friends of schools is that our work is not about "reform," it is about "renewal." John Goodlad sums it up best in his essay: "I hated the concept of school reform from the time of its emergence. . . . [Reform] is a nasty concept, defined by my Webster's dictionary as 'amendment of what is defective, vicious, corrupt, or depraved.' What an insult to throw at the stewards of schooling!" Our work is about the constant renewal of our schools. This is the lesson all five of these educators teach us. And that work never ends. We must continue to think about, as Goodlad puts it, schools "as they were, as they are, as they might become, and as they ought to be." The good school—and indeed the good community and nation—is always in the process of becoming what those before us only imagined and what those who will follow us will rethink and improve.

But to what end is a school to be a self-renewing enterprise? Across all these five lives, the word democracy is writ large. Thus, the second lesson is that the heart of public education, its most crucial mission, is to develop in the young the habits of heart and mind that make democracy possible. Against the oft-heard demands that the work of schools is to repair the economy or prepare students for college, these five have kept the flame of educating for democracy and citizenship alive. They see education as a campaign for equity and justice. As Ted Sizer relates in his essay, "education—ever more schooling—[is] the most likely vehicle to address the nation's pockets of poverty and racism." For these five, education is a calling—a calling to a higher purpose, a calling to make the democratic dream a reality through educating and empowering our children.

Which brings me to lesson three: democracy is not something we learn, it is something we do. Each of these five see schools as communities where we are, as one of my favorite colleagues puts it, "as democratic as we can stand to be." Hank Levin tells us that he sought to build schools "that enlisted a profoundly democratic process of building a unity of purpose, taking responsibility for decisions and their consequences, and building on the strengths of all of the participants including the students, teachers, other school staff, parents, and community members." Schools that prepare our future generations for the demands of democracy must also put those same demands upon themselves.

To do this, we must have faith in those closest to the children, teachers and parents. Deborah Meier has always held that faith close to her work. Her schools are places of deep collaboration between teachers, students, and families. As she has often reminded me, it is impossible for children to grow up to be powerful adults if they are in the company of adults who do not exercise such power themselves. Surrounding children with powerful adults and ensuring that their parents have power in the educational setting pushes back against the forces that would limit democratic participation. Yes, Meier notes, "poverty and racism have a powerful out-of-school impact on the lives of our children, which the school alone cannot 'undo.' In fact, undoing is not the task. The task of schools is to re-do schooling so that it meets the strengths that children of poverty bring with them, and joining with their families to make sure that schools are the richest and most soul and mind inspiring places they can be."

To do this means—and here is lesson number four—that renewing our schools is a systematic change. We cannot renew our schools by simply changing a curriculum, moving a teacher, or adding one more test. Rather, we must, as James Comer puts it, "focus first and primarily on the school as a system." How well I remember learning that lesson when I first became a school principal! The school I was heading was not very successful and was widely dismissed by the community. But it was populated with caring teachers and capable kids who were raised by parents who loved them. The issue was not the individuals in the school, the curriculum, or any one of the many other canards often cited as being the "problem" with schools. The problem was a systemic way of being organized that was designed to meet state guidelines and requirements but did little to reach the souls of our children or nurture the imagination of our staff. Changing the system, in spite of the sure-to-come critique of anyone or any thing who dares to be different, was necessary. And it was in the work and example of these five teachers that we found the courage to do what we ought to do.

We are still working at it. Reading the stories in this volume is a refreshing and inspiring reminder that renewal is on-going; that democracy demands all of our effort; that those who face the issues are most likely to have the best answers; and that it's the system, not the people, that always needs rethinking. So while the halls are quiet now, it is only a lull—a lull in which we are reconsidering our system, trying to figure out more ways to bring in families to inform our thinking, and, as is all too often the case, sorting out how to uphold our mission under the pressure of the state testing system.

There are so many more lessons to be learned from these five visionaries, lessons about how to live one's life in balance with other pursuits and enjoyments, lessons on how to view education from a multi-perspective set of lenses, lessons about how to handle leadership issues of funding and scaling, lessons about maneuvering in a political world, and so on. It is up to you, the reader, to cull your own lessons and to remember what brought you into this field and why the great expenditures of time and concern are all part of your path. These five visionaries have taught us that we should never settle for schools as they are but should always be creating better and fuller ways to educate children. This is the task that they have passed on to us, and in these pages they provide us with the necessary tools for this work, stories to inspire us along the way, and reminders as to why this path is so important.

And now there is one more lesson that I have learned for myself in reading this book. While I am not nearly as experienced as any of the five who dared, I have started to think about leaving the principal's desk I have occupied for the past 16 years. Perhaps, I think, a generation is long enough to impose yourself on any community. After all, within in a year I will start shaking the hands of children at graduation whose parents' hands I shook at the same ceremony not so long ago (it seems). But then I read these stories, and I realize that you never leave this work. I began here by expressing my concern that I had taken on too much when I agreed to write the conclusion for this book. But, upon reflection, I am delighted that I took Carl up on his invitation, because it reminded me that Ted, Deborah, James, Hank, and John are still at it. They are still standing boldly for schools that are not test factories but places that liberate the minds of our children and empower the adults who work with them. I am proud to be able to stand with them just a bit longer.

Suggested Reading

Jim Comer

Comer, J. P. (1989). *Maggie's American dream: The life and times of a Black family.* New York: Plume.

Comer, J. P. (1993). *School power: Implications of an intervention project.* New York: Free Press. (Original work published 1980)

Comer, J. P. (1997). *Waiting for a miracle: Why schools can't solve our problems and how we can.* New York: Dutton.

Comer, J. P. (2004). *Leave no child behind: Preparing today's youth for tomorrow's world.* New Haven, CT: Yale University Press.

Comer, J. P. (2005). Child and adolescent development: The critical missing focus in school reform. *Phi Delta Kappan, 86*(10), 757–763.

Darling-Hammond, L. (2005). *Preparing teachers for a changing world: What teachers should learn and be able to do.* San Francisco: Jossey-Bass.

Noblit, G. W., Malloy, C. E., & Malloy, W. (2001). *The kids got smarter: Case studies of successful Comer schools.* Cresskill, NJ: Hampton Press.

Carl Glickman

Glickman, C. D. (1993). *Renewing America's schools: A guide for school-based action.* San Francisco: Jossey-Bass.

Glickman, C. D. (1998). *Revolutionizing America's schools.* San Francisco: Jossey-Bass.

Glickman, C. D. (2002). *Leadership for learning.* Alexandria, VA: Association for Supervision and Curriculum Development.

Glickman, C. D. (2003). *Holding sacred ground: Courageous leadership for democratic schools.* San Francisco: Jossey-Bass.

Glickman, C. D. (Ed.). (2008). *Letters to the next president: What we can do about the real crisis in education* (2008 Election Edition). New York: Teachers College Press.

Glickman, C. D., Gordon, S., & Ross-Gordon, J. (2007). *Supervision and instructional leadership: A developmental approach* (7th ed.). Boston: Allyn and Bacon.

John Goodlad

Goodlad, J. I. (1979). *What schools are for*. Bloomington, IN: Phi Delta Kappa Educational Foundation. (Original work published 1979, 2nd edition in 1994, special signature edition with new preface and afterword for the PDK Centennial in 2006)

Goodlad, J. I. (1990). *Teachers for our nation's schools.* San Francisco: Jossey-Bass.

Goodlad, J. I. (1997). *In praise of education* (John Dewey lecture). New York: Teachers College Press.

Goodlad, J. I., Mantle-Bromley, C., & Goodlad, S. J. (2004). *Education for everyone: Agenda for education in a democracy.* San Francisco: Jossey-Bass.

Henry M. Levin

Dewey, J. (1997). *Experience and education.* New York: Touchstone. (Original work published by Simon and Schuster 1938)

Dewey, J. (2004). *Democracy and education.* Mineola, NY: Dover. (Original work published by Macmillan 1916)

Hopfenberg, W., Levin, H. M., Chase, C., Christensen, G., Moore, M., Soler, P., Brunner, I., Keller, B., & Rodriguez, G. (1993). *The accelerated schools resource guide.* San Francisco: Jossey-Bass.

Deborah Meier

Duckworth, E. (2006). *"The having of wonderful ideas" and other essays on teaching and learning* (3rd ed.). New York: Teachers College Press.

Rose, M. (1999). *Lives on the boundary: The struggles and achievements of America's underprepared.* New York: Touchstone.

Rose, M. (2005). *The mind at work: Valuing the intelligence of the American worker.* New York: Penguin.

Rothstein, R. (1998). *The way we were? The myths and realities of America's student achievement* (Century Foundation/Twentieth Century Fund Report). New York: Century Foundation Press.

Sizer, T. (1985). *Horace's compromise: The dilemma of the American high school.* New York: Houghton Mifflin.

Weber, L. (1997). *Looking back and thinking forward: Reexaminations of teaching and schooling.* New York: Teachers College Press.

Ted Sizer

Adler, M. J. (1982). *The paideia proposal: An educational manifesto.* New York: Collier.

Gardner, H. (1991). *The disciplined mind.* New York: Basic Books.

Perkins, D. (1992). *Smart schools.* New York: Free Press.

Powell, A. G., Farrar, E., & Cohen, D. K. (1985). *The shopping mall high school.* Boston: Beacon Press.

Sizer, T. R., & Sizer, N. F. (1999). *The students are watching.* Boston: Beacon Press.

George Wood

Meier, D., & Wood, G. H. (Eds.). (2004). *Many children left behind: How the No Child Left Behind Act is damaging our children and our schools.* Boston: Beacon.

Wood, G. H. (1993). *Schools that work: America's most innovative public education programs.* New York: Plume.

Wood, G. H. (1999). *Time to learn: The story of one high school's remarkable transformation and the people who made it happen.* New York: Plume.